CONSIDERING
Others

Good Manners to Glorify God

A Biblical and Practical
Parental Guide
to Good Manners

CONSIDERING
Others

Good Manners to Glorify God

A Biblical and Practical
Parental Guide
to Good Manners

JUNGU OLOBIA

Published by Redemption Press, PO Box 427, Enumclaw, WA 98022
Toll Free (844) 2REDEEM (273-3336)

Redemption Press is honored to present this title in partnership with the author. The views expressed or implied in this work are those of the author. Redemption Press provides our imprint seal representing design excellence, creative content and high quality production.

ISBN 13: 978-1-68314-623-0
ePub ISBN: 978-1-68314-624-7
Kindle ISBN: 978-1-68314-625-4
Library of Congress Catalog Card Number: 2018965753

This book is dedicated to the Holy Spirit,
for the development of godly character,
integrity, and success in children
of all ages everywhere.

Foreword

Considering Others: Good Manners to Glorify God is a book we believe has been long needed. It is not just another book full of tips and points on etiquette, but much more. We live in a season where justification for what we do and how we do it begs for correctness, and in some cases reverence. Jungu Olobia has poured her time and heart into sharing with people of all ages the importance of manners and behavior through the principles as defined and described in the living Word of God. She addresses matters of life that affect the smallest to the eldest of persons.

As Christian parents, we are often faced with the balance between society's guidelines and what the Bible has to say on how to conduct oneself in any situation. Jungu has done a great job in applying Scripture to every area of behavior and manners and brings light to the important role they play in one's destiny.

Children are impressionable, and their characters are molded at a young age. We personally can recall that much of our etiquette and manners were shaped by not just our parents but the godly influences in our lives. There was always the reminder that first, we represent Christ, and second, we were always to be ready for whatever situation or environment we would find ourselves in. The chapters in the book on the role parents and guardians play in influencing and molding their children's lives are so important to understand and embrace. The Word of God tells us in Deuteronomy 11 that it is our responsibility to teach the Word of God to our children at all times and in all situations. This book supports and reinforces the teachings of God's Word.

So a big God bless and kudos to Sister Jungu Olobia for her obedience to God and allowing Him to use her to address this very important subject.

Pastors Stephen R. and Emilia Hill

Table of Contents

Introduction

The idea for this book began in October 2015, when one of my pastors, Pastor Emilia Hill, asked me to put together a ten-minute segment on etiquette for a "children's tea" she'd envisioned for the children at our church. By that time, I had been serving for about twelve years as a volunteer teacher in the children's church—about seven years at my previous church in Pittsburgh, Pennsylvania, and about five years at my current church in Southlake, Texas.

My two children, Andrew and Joshua, were seven and two and a half years of age, respectively, in 2015. I proudly remember one Sunday morning a few years before, Andrew—five years old then—asked me and the head usher if he could serve as an usher. Since then, he has been serving as a junior usher. Pastor Emilia and many others have often complimented my husband and me on our children's good manners, so when she asked that I teach the children about etiquette, I gladly accepted.

As I prepared my etiquette presentation, something amazing happened: Scriptures flooded my mind. The Holy Spirit taught me that etiquette and good manners have always been God's idea first. I realized that the Bible is truly God's etiquette, a life manual for righteous, victorious, and successful living. Titus 3:1–2 (ISV): "Remind believers to submit to rulers and authorities, to be obedient, and to be ready to do any honorable kind of work. They are not to insult anyone or be argumentative. Instead, they are to be gentle and perfectly courteous to everyone."

The foundation for respectful behavior is the Word of God. The way we treat one another matters. Etiquette may be different between cultures; however, practicing good manners is a kindness that extends across cultures. We honor people from other countries or backgrounds by honoring each other's etiquette. Many relationships in marriages, families, churches, businesses, and governments fail because of poor interpersonal (social) and communication (interactional) skills. Education, talents and gifts, connections, appearance, and money are important in our world; however, time and time again we see—and studies show—that the key to true success is how we interact with one another. In other words, how we speak to and about each other (verbal interaction) and how we behave around each other (physical interaction) are the golden keys. Taking time to learn and understand etiquette and good manners will help us build better personal and professional relationships. Good manners and etiquette will open doors where education, beauty, money, or power cannot.

Psalm 34:11–14 (NLT): "Come, my children, and listen to me, and I will teach you to fear the Lord. Does anyone want to live a life that is long and prosperous? Then keep your tongue from speaking evil and your lips from telling lies! Turn away from evil and do good. Search for peace, and work to maintain it." Let us take a moment to meditate on the richness of these Scriptures. In verse 11 we are alerted, warned even, that there may be many who are called God's children, but only those who truly listen will be taught to fear the Lord.

Fearing the Lord is something that must be taught. This is one of the reasons why it is vital that every believer belong to a Bible-believing local church where they can be taught the Word of God and grow in spiritual understanding and wisdom. To be taught, we must be willing to listen. As I continue to meditate on verse 11, allowing the Word of God to judge my heart, I tremble as I ask this question: Am I listening to the Holy Spirit, my Teacher? If I am, is there any evidence of this? What fruit do I exhibit? The Bible tells us in Galatians 5:22–23 (NLT): "But the Holy Spirit produces this kind of fruit in our lives: love, joy, peace, patience, kindness, goodness, faithfulness, gentleness, and self-control. There is no law against these things!" From this foundation we can develop good manners.

What are bad manners? Simply put, bad manners are bad habits or behaviors. They are demonstrated by the following:

1. A bad attitude
2. Being disrespectful and unkind to others
3. Talking back to parents and other elders
4. Unwilling to listen and obey God-appointed authority, such as parents and teachers
5. Incessantly interrupting when others are speaking
6. Unwilling to forgive, bitter and vengeful (I will punish you my own way to hurt you so that I feel better.)
7. Emotionally unstable, temperamental, abusive to humans and animals
8. Suspicious and falsely accusing to control and manipulate situations
9. Lazy, unwilling to help out
10. Impatient (I want it and I want now!)
11. Bullying—including cyberbullying—fighting, hitting, harassing, and secretly betraying others, believing the lie that what they do not know will not hurt them
12. Envious (I don't want it, but I don't want you to have it.)
13. Jealous (I want it, and I want to take it from you so you won't have it.)

14. Slanderous (spreading embarrassing truths or lies about others to destroy their reputations, even under the guise of praying for them with the intention of appearing more righteous. Also included here is online defamation via social media.)

15. Every bad and unwholesome speech and deed, including breaking the laws of the land

This list depicts negative human choices, but if we are being led by the Holy Spirit and listening to Him, we are called, instead, per Psalm 34:13–14 (NLT) to "keep [our] tongue from speaking evil and [our] lips from telling lies. [To] turn away from evil and do good. To search for peace, and work to maintain it." This takes effort. It takes learning etiquette and good manners God's way.

Chapter 1

Good Manners Save the Day

A fool vents all of his anger, but a wise
man brings himself under control.
(PROVERBS 29:11 WEB)

Brave, wise, considerate, and kind. That's how the author of 1 Samuel described a beautiful woman named Abigail. In contrast, her husband, Nabal, is described as extremely harsh, evil, mean, cruel, and badly behaved. While Abigail was graced with godly wisdom and excellent manners, it's clear that her husband, Nabal, though prosperous, didn't value the same things as his wife. Let's take a closer look at the biblical story in 1 Samuel 25 about these two characters and the consequences of their choices.

Nabal was a wealthy but arrogant man who owned thousands of sheep and goats. The Bible discloses that to many in his community, he was infamously known to be hot tempered, vulgar, stubborn, insensitive, abusive, a fool, defiant, dishonest, corrupt, cursed, an embarrassment to his Calebite tribe, and so evil and arrogant that no one could speak to him. Sadly, these labels represent many in our world today, both young and old, both lay worker and leader, both Christian and non-Christian.

These descriptions of Nabal's character were expressed by many publicly and privately, including by members of his own household: his wife, Abigail, and his male servant. The people who know us best, who see our true character, are God and members of our families. Nabal was a husband, a successful businessman, a leader in the community with many servants, a neighbor, a citizen of Israel, which also means he was supposed to be a believer and doer of God's Word. Being so indifferent, cruel, and complacent was something he learned from an early age, something he perfected over time and with much practice.

David and his men had been camping in the wilderness where Nabal's men grazed the livestock, and David's group had protected Nabal's from danger day and night. After some time, during a holiday season, David heard Nabal was shearing his sheep. (Here is the significance of shearing sheep: My grandparents had a large farm in Kenya, where they raised sheep and other livestock. During holidays and other special family occasions, they would slaughter a sheep or goat to prepare as part of a great feast. Before they slaughtered the sheep, they sheared it. It was the same with Nabal.) David understood that shearing meant it was time for slaughter, time for celebration, which meant there would be plenty of fresh meat to enjoy. He immediately sent ten young men to Nabal requesting provisions, as they had not harmed his workers or stolen his animals—in fact, they had protected them.

Why ten? Ten was a nonthreatening number to show that David came in peace, that he understood order and respect, and that he was not greedy, even if he had six hundred soldiers, not including their families and servants, to feed. The number ten also points to God's perfect timing and order, completeness or fullness of time. For example, we have the Ten Commandments. There were ten plagues of judgment upon Egypt, causing them to release, though reluctantly, the Israelites from slavery. The number ten perhaps represented God's completions of goodness and mercy toward Nabal. He gave him one more opportunity to repent of his evil ways. The Bible also points out that David sent young men. The significance of young men may be that even if Nabal and Abigail had no children together, they still had the opportunity to influence other people's children, by showing them what hospitality, kindness, grace, and mercy look like.

Not knowing how ungrateful, unscrupulous, and insolent Nabal was, David instructed his messengers to exercise protocol before this leader by speaking a blessing over Nabal before asking for anything. When the ten young men met with Nabal, they relayed David's blessing for long life, peace upon him and his family, and continued increase of everything that Nabal owned. David humbled himself through these young men, even calling himself a son of Nabal, for he said in verse 1 Samuel 25:8: "Ask your young men; they will tell you this is true [that we stole nothing; instead, we protected your servants and possessions]. Please return our kindness and look on my young men with favor since we come on this feast day. Please give whatever you can spare to them and to your son David" (*Voice*).

David offering himself as a son let Nabal know that he was extending a hand of lifelong friendship, loyalty, protection, favor, love, and respect. Nabal, however, was too blinded by vanity and a false reality of himself. Well known for his hot temper, he reacted to David's kindness and humility with utter contempt, verbalizing grave insults and foolish threats for David and his men. He arrogantly refused to honor David's request, calling David an unknown defiant, runaway slave who was leading a gang of insurgents. These were serious insults because Nabal not only rejected David, but despised, as if nothing,

David and his men's personal sacrifices, great victories, and loyalties to King Saul and the nation of Israel.

The young men immediately departed to inform David, who became infuriated and decided to avenge himself and his soldiers. Immediately arming himself, he called for four hundred of his men to arms as well and descended toward Nabal's estate to execute him and his entire household.

Four hundred is a large number and of great significance, for it reminds us of bondage, afflictions, idolatry, trials, and even fulfillment of prophecy. For example, God tells Abraham that the Israelites would be in slavery for four hundred years in Egypt but promises they would be released and possess Canaan. The number four hundred also refers to death and the grave. For example, after the death of Sarah, Abraham purchases land from the Hittites for four hundred shekels of silver as a burial site for his beloved wife. In Nabal's case, terrible judgment was sure because of his continued obstinacy. Proverbs 29:1 (TPT): "Stubborn people who repeatedly refuse to accept correction will suddenly be broken and never recover."

In 1 Samuel 25:14, one of the male servants informed Abigail of her husband's harsh and foolish actions against David's men and ultimately against his own household, encouraging her to act quickly, for David had planned immediate retaliation. Abigail was horrified, understanding the dangerous repercussions of her husband's foolishness, for who had not heard of David's bravery and great success in battle against the enemies of Israel? Without delay, Abigail concocts a quick and brilliant plan to save her family and servants from sure death. She hurriedly packs and loads up her donkeys with hundreds of food provisions for David and his men and informed her servants to go ahead of her. How brilliant and wise! The sight of the gifts would have appeased David and his men enough to allow Abigail the opportunity to apologize and explain the situation. Proverbs 18:16 (*Voice*): "The *right* gift *at the right time* can open up new opportunities and gains access to influential people."

Deciding it best not to inform or alert her husband, Abigail left his estate to approach and appease David herself. As she was riding down the mountain on a hidden trail, she suddenly came upon an angry David and his men on their way to destroy her home. She immediately dismounted from her donkey and fell at David's feet, apologizing profusely for her husband's foolish and arrogant words against him and his men. Abigail reminded David that God would surely avenge his enemies and that her hot-tempered husband was not worth shedding any blood over. She proved to David she was nothing like her husband by letting him know she did not see the messengers he had sent and that she even prayed that all of David's enemies become cursed, as Nabal was.

Abigail demonstrates godly wisdom and understanding when she reminded David of God's blessings, protection, and promises concerning his life. She ended with a request that when the Lord had fulfilled those promises, that David please remember her. Abigail then presented her gifts to David, who accepted them and her apology, his anger having been appeased. He immediately changed his mind about killing Nabal and his entire household, acknowledging, thanking, and blessing Abigail for her discernment and tactfulness.

Abigail returned home to find her husband partying like a king and heavily drunk. She waited till the morning, when her husband had sobered up, to tell him what happened the day before. On hearing the news, Nabal had a stroke and lay paralyzed in bed. Ten or so days later, the Lord took his life.

David heard the news of Nabal's death and rejoiced that the Lord kept him from avenging himself by killing Nabal. Without delay, awed by Abigail's humility, decorum, and wittiness, David sent messengers to her with a marriage proposal, which she gladly accepted, leaving with them to become David's wife. All this because of kind and pleasant words and actions.

From the story, we see the consequences of bad manners in that Nabal lost everything in the end, including his wife, his wealth and estate, and even his life. He had no interest in considering others and was hated and despised by many, including his own wife. Notice that though Abigail was married to him, because of his bad temper and stubbornness, she chose to keep pertinent information from him. This is a warning to those who neglect and abuse their spouses and children, that eventually they will lose everything. Nabal lacked good sense and did not get to enjoy the blessings of the Lord for long.

After Nabal's death, and with David's marriage proposal, Abigail did not hesitate to leave Nabal's wealth, estate, and many servants. She left everything behind except for five female attendants who accompanied her to her new home. Many times, the number five in the Bible refers to grace, favor, freedom, and provision. For example, the boy with the five loaves and two fish that Jesus miraculously multiplied to feed thousands of people. In Exodus 20:12, the fifth commandment is the only commandment, out of the ten, with a promise: "Honor your father and mother. Then you will live a long, full life in the land the Lord your God is giving you" (NLT).

Abigail demonstrated understanding in good manners. She showed good manners when she apologized for what her husband had done, and blessed David, persuading him to repent of his plans to annihilate her family. Abigail demonstrated good etiquette when she stepped up to the plate, taking the difficult responsibility of providing food provisions for David and his men, something that was her husband's responsibility. She showed great consideration for others when she put herself in danger by approaching David, and his four-hundred mighty-men army, so that others could be saved, hence abating disaster on all sides.

Having been born and raised in Kenya, I have seen how many use wealth and power to destroy others, especially when there is no law and order to protect the poor, to protect women, and to protect children. Yet God is still there, and a defender and avenger of the oppressed, especially when they call on Him. When we look at ourselves and our society today, what kind of example are we to others: our children, our spouses, our neighbors, our coworkers?

As a mother, I care deeply about raising and training my children to have godly character. Just as Abigail was appalled by her husband's behavior, I am appalled by the total lack of respect and lack of consideration for others rampant in our world today. Every kind of crime, including cyberbullying, identity thefts, and hackings are at an all-time high. I worked at a college for ten years and witnessed firsthand the shocking and disrespectful behavior of some of our youth. We only need turn on the news, read a newspaper, or talk to our children, a teacher, a policeman, a coworker, or a neighbor to hear something troubling about someone hurting another.

We live in a world that is cutthroat, where the end justifies the means and collateral damage is the order of the day. We hear of high-collar crimes and golden parachutes, and we wonder how people can live with themselves knowing they've lost or stolen millions of pension funds and destroyed countless lives. We hear of the pure evil and carnage of terrorists around the world, the wars and rumors of wars, and wonder how some can have so much hatred. Abigail, a wealthy woman and employer of many with her husband, cared for her employees. She did not have children with Nabal, yet she risked her life for her servants by approaching an angry war general and not only humbling herself before him but also before his soldiers and even before her own servants.

My husband has been practicing pediatric medicine for over twenty-five years, seeing newborn babies to eighteen-year-olds, and the alcohol and drug epidemic among the youth is staggering, especially the percentage from broken homes. There are many cases of horrifying abuse by parents, other relatives, and mentors against their children. There are also terrible abuses by children against children at home and in school. Statistics show that more children are being exposed to pornography from an early age and that they act out what they see by sometimes even preying on other children. In 2016 the American College of Pediatricians, a national medical association of licensed physicians and healthcare professionals, released an article entitled "The Impact of Media Use and Screen Time on Children, Adolescents, and Families," which stated:

> A recent and systematic examination of the peer-reviewed research spanning years 1995 to 2015 indicated that pornography use among adolescents is prevalent, mainly accessed via the Internet, and first exposure often occurs unintentionally. Although there are many variables impacting this research, pornography is associated with more permissive sexual attitudes and stronger gender-stereotypical sexual beliefs. Additionally, the same review found pornography used to be associated with early sexual intercourse, greater experience with casual sex behavior, and increased sexual aggression both as perpetrators and victims.

Other concerns in society are increasing problems with homelessness, mental health issues, abductions, child soldiering, and human smuggling and trafficking, which are all at an all-time high. Second Timothy 3:1–5 (KJV): "This know also, that in the last days perilous times shall come. For men shall be lovers of their own selves, covetous, boasters, proud, blasphemers, disobedient to parents, unthankful, unholy, Without natural affection, trucebreakers, false accusers, incontinent, fierce, despisers of those that are good, Traitors, heady, highminded, lovers of pleasures more than lovers of God; Having a form of godliness, but denying the power thereof: from such turn away."

To start the process for healing, it is important to recognize we have a serious problem in our world today. The solution to the problem is believing in and wholeheartedly following the example of Jesus Christ. There is no other way. Christ is God's answer to a terribly troubled world. With salvation comes the gift of the Holy Spirit, who teaches us God's Truth (the Bible) and God's way of living, first by loving Him, then, second, by loving our neighbor.

Who is my neighbor? My neighbor is anyone who needs my help. Who needs my help? As a wife, my husband needs my help, for he is my immediate neighbor, followed by my children. It's important to prioritize who's and what's truly important to nurture healthy marriages and families.

Pay attention to the amount of time spent browsing the internet, or working, or playing hobbies, or with friends and colleagues, or playing video games, or on social media, such as Facebook and Twitter, compared to the time we spend with our families. It's so easy to end up ignoring, neglecting, and abandoning family members and not realizing it until it's too late.

Technology addictions are major problems around the world today. In South Korea, for example, there is a law forbidding youth under the age of sixteen from playing online video games between midnight and 6:00 a.m. The "shutdown law," also called the "Cinderella law," went into effect in 2011. Access to online games is blocked during the shutdown period for all gamers under sixteen.

It's clear we need help overcoming technology addictions. That help starts by humbling ourselves, repenting before a holy God, and calling on Him for direction. We need to obey His instructions as parents and guardians—then we will be successful in training our children in godliness and integrity.

In 1 Samuel 25:18, we see Abigail's response to serious trouble. She understood the dire consequences of her husband's foolishness. "Then Abigail, *knowing the stakes*, rushed about gathering *gifts similar to what her husband should have offered*: 200 loaves, 2 jugs of wine, 5 sheep (butchered and dressed), more than 50 quarts of roasted grain, 100 clusters of raisins, and 200 fig cakes. She had these loaded on donkeys" (*Voice*). She looked foolishness, rage, and death in the face and took them down single handedly with humility, repentance, kindness of speech, and generosity. Abigail was resolute, fearless, and focused on what needed to be done. She carried the burden of blame herself rather than command one of her many servants to do the deed. This is what it will take to save our children—it will take individuals who realize we cannot be complacent and must take on the responsibility of building up our own families, our marriages, our children with the Word of God and the Holy Spirit as our guide.

Additional Reflection Verse

Proverbs 11:29 (*Voice*): A person who stirs up trouble in his family will inherit stormy winds, and foolish troublers will end up serving the wise.

Chapter 2

Developing Good Manners, Etiquette, and Protocol

*A gracious man benefits himself, but the
cruel person damages himself.*
(**PROVERBS 11:17 ISV**)

As a Sunday school teacher for over sixteen years, I've had the wonderful opportunity of teaching biblical principles to children from three to twelve years old. My observations and experiences in the children's ministry have helped me understand what good manners really are and why we need them so desperately in our society today. Children learn from their parents and surroundings on how to be kind and respectful. I've realized that truly, we as parents and guardians have a God-given responsibility to train up our children in the way they should be. It's not something that happens automatically. It takes work—daily prayer, daily studying the Word of God, setting healthy boundaries, and surrounding ourselves with wise like-minded people for support.

My boys are now ten and six, and I love to hear from others how well mannered they are at school, at church, at the store, everywhere we go. They are happy, healthy, and flourishing, as all children should. Yes, there are tears and lots of repetitive training at home, but when I see them willingly serving the homeless, the church, and the community, and praying for others, I rejoice. I have a deep longing to help other parents, and so with much prayer and encouragement from my pastors, I wrote this book for the godly training up of all children worldwide.

What is the difference between good manners, etiquette, and protocol?

Good Manners

Good manners are behaviors that show we respect ourselves and others. They reveal character, temperament, and upbringing. Bad manners reveal selfishness, unruliness, and disregard for others. Demonstrating good manners means we are respectful, truthful, and kind. Good manners promote healthy interactions in every aspect of society: in family, business, government, or any other social function including social media. Genuine good manners come from God. Galatians 5:22–23 (WEB): "But the fruit of the Spirit is love, joy, peace, patience, kindness, goodness, faith, gentleness, and self-control. Against such things there is no law."

Etiquette

While good manners answer the questions of what we are to say or do and to whom, etiquette answers the questions of why, how, and when we say or do something. Etiquette is the rules of a culture that tell us why, how, and when manners should be expressed in a social setting. For example, we know it is good manners to say "Thank you" and "Please." However, etiquette tells us when we should say "thank you" and when we should say "Please." For example, I have taught my children what good manners to use when someone pays them a compliment. They practice good etiquette when they give the correct response: "Thank you" (and not "Please").

Knowing and understanding etiquette demonstrates good training. Etiquette training begins at home and continues with experience or through research and help of an expert. Parents and guardians play a critical role in training children to have etiquette. Part of that training includes discipline to correct bad or disrespectful behavior.

The purpose of etiquette is to produce citizens who understand socially acceptable behaviors in their society. When we know how we are supposed to conduct ourselves in various settings, then peace, harmony, confidence, and (in many cases) acceptance are the results. There are many types of etiquette, including social etiquette, dinner etiquette, family etiquette, business etiquette, technology etiquette, phone etiquette, and flag etiquette.

The rules for etiquette change when we cross national borders. However, while etiquette may change across borders and from culture to culture, good manners are more cross cultural and transnational. Remember Nabal, Abigail, and David? Nabal belonged to the tribe of Caleb, while David was from the tribe of Judah. These were unique tribes with distinct cultural differences. Everyone involved in the story represents a different role, point of view, gender, age group, and different social and economic experience. In Kenya, for example, there are almost seventy tribes that speak their own unique language, have their own staple food, way of dress, style of dance, music, and other unique practices. Regardless of the tribal cultural differences, I learned to recognize, appreciate, and respect individuals with good sense and discernment.

Taking time to learn and understand good manners, etiquette, and protocol, will help us build better personal and professional relationships, and open more doors than education, beauty, money, or power ever could.

Dinner etiquette in the United States is different from dinner etiquette in Japan, where they use chopsticks instead of a fork and knife. Also, it is considered extremely rude in Japan to show up for dinner at a restaurant without a reservation. When entering a Japanese home, remove your shoes and greet guests with a slight bow. There should be no talking or shaking of hands; instead sit silently until addressed. In Kenya, dinner etiquette is different: at the door, the guest may not necessarily knock, but instead say in Swahili, "*Hodi!*" (ho-dee), meaning "Greetings! May I come in?" The host then responds while opening the door, "*Karibu!*" meaning "Welcome!" Hands are shaken with lots of jubilant conversation that includes gratitude, compliments, and blessings all around. Later we will discuss in detail more practical tips for etiquette.

Due to globalization and advancements in technology, it has become paramount to learn and understand etiquette for successful integration into different cultures and nations. Many political and business negotiations falter due to a lack of understanding in etiquette, protocol, and manners. For example, in many nonwestern cultures, business and political talks are not conducted until after a lengthy hearty meal and an exchange of pleasantries and gifts. This is the case in Asian, African, and Middle Eastern countries. Members of these nations want a "feel" of your character before signing a contract. They want to observe if it's just about the money and numbers or if you're also prudent and respectful enough of their culture.

Learn international etiquette before traveling for business or vacation. Carry a dictionary or download a translation app for the language of the nation you're visiting. No matter how dire of a state some nations are in, always start with gratitude and appreciation by stating something honest and complimentary, such as the beautiful scenery or artwork, the delicious cuisine, etc. Also, know and respect the laws of the country. For example, loud, obnoxious, illegal, or immoral behavior is frowned upon by many. Follow the respectful behavior of the host. Expect and make room for long social events and travel before signing any contract. These may seem corrupt, unnecessary, and a total waste of time to some, but the efforts of learning and respecting others and their cultures will go a long way and win you respect, trustworthiness, friendship, credibility, and what you travel to that country for. Wars have been abated over meals and nations saved by the exchange of gifts and pleasant words. Abigail reminds us of that.

Protocol

Protocol is different from good manners and etiquette. It refers to rules that guide interaction with dignitaries. It also refers to rules that guide the behavior of dignitaries, politicians, and other government officials as they interact with each other. Scripture shows correct protocol in prayer when coming before our heavenly Father, the King of kings. Psalm 100:4 (WEB): "Enter into his gates with thanksgiving, into his courts with praise. Give thanks to him, and bless his name." Coming into a court signals we are coming before someone of authority, royalty, and greatness. These Scriptures reveal God as King and Judge. Correct protocol to get His attention dictates we start with thanksgiving for all His goodness, mercy, and favor toward us. Next, we give God praise, demonstrating we recognize His greatness, excellence, and might. After this, we present our gifts before Him. These acts of love bring great delight to the Lord because they show we trust, appreciate, and recognize His great love for us.

Having good manners means choosing to do and say kind and respectful things even when others do not. It means putting others first. According to Luke 6:45, what we say flows from what is in our heart. Showing good manners means we care about how we communicate in speech and deed. How do I sound to another person when I speak? My words, expressions, and behavior, do they promote peace and unity, or do they promote discomfort and disunity?

Having good manners means showing mercy and compassion to the hearers of our words and the viewers of our behavior. In unsettling situations, we learn to show kindness, respect, and restraint by controlling what we say and how we say it. Having spiritual understanding and maturity will help us to not be so easily offended. We learn to forgive and let go. We choose to extend mercy and grace to others, including difficult people and in difficult situations. Proverbs 19:11 (WEB): "The discretion of a man makes him slow to anger. It is his glory to overlook an offense."

As I continue to grow in my Christian faith, I have learned who my real enemy is—Satan. My spouse, my children, my brothers and sisters in the faith, and all other people are not the real enemy. The father of all lies, deception, strife, unbelief, doubt, hate, prejudice, immorality, confusion, depression, and all other evil is Satan. Scripture is clear that we have an invisible enemy who seeks to steal, kill, and destroy us. It is important we understand how to fight for our marriages, our children and everything that concerns them, the church body, our leaders and the decisions they make, and the rest of the world. We fight unseen evil forces through prayer and obedience to God's Word. It's also important to stay planted in a local Bible-believing church so that we may be encouraged, especially during the many challenges and trials of life.

More than ever, we need love and compassion for others. Compassion is a gift that comes from the Creator, for He is Love. To receive it, we must ask for it. James 1:17 (ERV): "Everything good comes from God. Every perfect gift is from him. These good gifts come down from the Father who made all the lights in the sky. But God never changes like the shadows from those lights. He is always the same." There is a condition when asking God for something, and that is we must believe that He is willing and able to do what we ask Him to do. James 1:5–8 (WEB): "But if any of you lacks wisdom, let him ask of God, who gives to all liberally and without reproach; and it will be given to him. But let him ask in faith, without any doubting, for he who doubts is like a wave of the sea, driven by the wind and tossed. For let that man not think that he will receive anything from the Lord. He is a double-minded man, unstable in all his ways."

As we depend on the Holy Spirit and obey God's Word by showing love and extending grace, our children can change their world by practicing good manners, etiquette, and protocol.

An amazing truth: Children are the greatest in the kingdom of heaven, and so it goes without saying that God cares how children are treated and raised on earth. They are, after all, the leaders of today and tomorrow. Leaders come from the people. They are a product of their families and communities. Hosea 4:9 (WEB): "It will be, like people, like priest; and I will punish them for their ways, and will repay them for their deeds." The kind of leaders we get and want as spouses, parents, friends, colleagues, bosses, pastors, politicians, business partners, and so forth will be determined by the example they see and hear and by the upbringing and instruction they receive when young. Children today, leaders tomorrow, fully equipped to love others through good manners, etiquette, and protocol.

Additional Reflection Verses

Proverbs 15:1 (WEB): A gentle answer turns away wrath, but a harsh word stirs up anger.

Proverbs 16:23 (BBE): The heart of the wise man is the teacher of his mouth, and gives increased learning to his lips.

Proverbs 18:11 (*Voice*): The rich *think their* wealth is their sturdy fortress; they imagine it to be an invincible wall *of security*.

Proverbs 29:22 (WEB) An angry man stirs up strife, and a wrathful man abounds in sin.

Luke 6:45 (KJV): A good man out of the good treasure of his heart bringeth forth that which is good; and an evil man out of the evil treasure of his heart bringeth forth that which is evil: for of the abundance of the heart his mouth speaketh.

Ephesians 4:2–3 (*Voice*): Be humble. Be gentle. Be patient. Tolerate one another in *an atmosphere thick with* love. Make every effort to preserve the unity the Spirit has already created, with peace binding you together.

Chapter 3
The Holy Spirit, Our Guide

Early in the morning, while it was still dark,
he rose up and went out, and departed into
a deserted place, and prayed there.
(MARK 1:35 WEB)

The same Spirit who was with Jesus and other godly individuals is the Spirit of God, who is with every obedient believer in Christ. Daniel, the great prophet and loyal advisor to several Babylonian kings, said that those who know their God would do great exploits. In the book of Daniel, we see the mighty work of the Holy Spirit in the lives of four captive Hebrew preteen or teen children, guiding them with such wisdom, integrity, grace, poise, and courage in a dark and dangerous society. The Holy Spirit taught and guided them on protocol with their captors so much so that they believed Daniel to have the spirit of their gods. God had given King Nebuchadnezzar of Babylon victory against the king of Judah, seizing him as prisoner while taking the royal family and other nobility captive. This all happened because the people of

God refused to listen to God's many warnings to abandon false gods and turn back to Him wholeheartedly.

The Babylonians expected their captives to assimilate by embracing every aspect of the Babylonian culture, including being renamed as Babylonians. Certain pagan expectations and requirements were a serious problem for Daniel and his friends, as they did not want to violate God's laws by defiling themselves with non-kosher foods that had been dedicated to Babylonian gods. The Babylonians were an extremely ruthless and feared people, yet Daniel determined not to eat the king's rich foods and wine. Instead he requested of the chief eunuch, Ashpenaz, that he be excused so as not to defile himself. Without the strength of the Holy Spirit, it is impossible to stand up for righteousness like Daniel did in the face of persecutions. First Corinthians 12:3 (ESV): "Therefore I want you to understand that no one speaking in the Spirit of God ever says, 'Jesus is accursed!' and no one can say 'Jesus is Lord' except in the Holy Spirit."

God had given Daniel special favor with Ashpenaz. However, Ashpenaz was too concerned that the king might punish him and so declined Daniel's request. Daniel turned to the steward over them and pleaded with him to test them for ten days on a diet of only vegetables and water, and he agreed. After ten days, the steward examined the young men and found Daniel and his friends much healthier and better looking than the noble young men of other lands. After three years of training, King Nebuchadnezzar interviewed them and found them to be ten times better than their counterparts, so each became an important official in the king's court. Daniel continued to serve as a high official, advising four kings of Babylon: Nebuchadnezzar, Belshazzar, Darius, and Cyrus. The godly character, courage, wise counsel, and tact of the Hebrew young men impressed and influenced the Babylonian kings and their governments. King Cyrus released the

Israelites from captivity and financed the rebuilding of the temple in Jerusalem.

God gave Daniel and his friends superior intelligence to understand all forms of learning, plus incredible wisdom, as rewards for their faithfulness and bravery. God gave Daniel an additional gift: the ability to interpret visions and dreams. As the young Hebrew men honored God by using their God-given gifts, many lives were spared from death, including their own. One such occasion occurred when King Nebuchadnezzar had a troubling dream and called for the magicians, sorcerers, astrologers, and enchanters of Babylon to tell him the dream and interpret it also. They were unable to do so, and this greatly infuriated the king, who ordered the execution of all the wise men of Babylon.

The Bible tells us that when Arioch, the commander of the king's guard, was sent out to execute the death decree, Daniel spoke to him with wisdom and diplomacy. Arioch then told him the reason the king had given such a harsh order. Once again, we see that good manners paid of here; otherwise, it's possible that Daniel and his friends could have lost their lives that very moment. The Babylonians were a dangerous and ruthless people.

To have good manners, we need the wisdom of God. Daniel came before the king and asked for time to seek his God for revelation and interpretation and was granted his request. That night, together with his three friends, Daniel cried out to the Lord for mercy, and God answered their request. Daniel informed Arioch, who immediately took him and came before the king to reveal and interpret the dream. The pagan king was in such awe that he responded by thanking and worshiping the Lord. First Corinthians 12:7 (*Voice*): "Each believer has received a gift that manifests the Spirit's *power and presence*. That gift is given for the good of the whole community."

Daniel and his friends had strong relationships with God because of the godly families they came from, where they were taught to revere and trust God. Daniel unashamedly prayed three times a day and regularly fasted, which gave him strength to endure and remain steadfast even when threatened with death many times. His three friends were the same: though threatened with being burned alive in a furnace, they refused to bow down to a Babylonian idol. These youth lived to honor God and His people. Throughout his life, Daniel never failed to mention to all that it was God who had given him the abilities to interpret dreams and give prophecies. Because of this, we see the miraculous work of the Holy Spirit throughout Daniel's life as he served God and others. Like Abigail, God gave Daniel wisdom and understanding to solve impossible problems with grace, consideration, and following established protocol.

Who is the Holy Spirit? Jesus said in John 14:26–27 (KJV), "But the Comforter, which is the Holy Ghost, whom the Father will send in my name, he shall teach you all things, and bring all things to your remembrance, whatsoever I have said unto you. Peace I leave with you, my peace I give unto you: not as the world giveth, give I unto you. Let not your heart be troubled, neither let it be afraid." For believers and followers of Christ, the Holy Spirit is our great and true Teacher, our Reminder of Scripture, our Comforter—bringing us peace of mind and heart. He is our Advocate—pleading for us like a seasoned, unbeatable lawyer before our heavenly Father. The Holy Spirit is our great Intercessor—crying out and communicating through us to King Jesus and the Father with bull's-eye discernment, precision, and perfect intercession. There is no one like Him. There is no match on earth or in the heavens that can be compared to His humility, companionship, trustworthiness, creativity, guidance, or protection. He stands alone as the great and undefeated champion of all ages.

How do we seek the Holy Spirit for guidance in the area of good manners? Everyone has weaknesses or things that can easily distract, so in my case the first thing I do is turn off the TV if it's on and silence the phone and computer or iPad, and then I go to a quiet place alone. Going to a quiet place is following the example of Christ when He retreated from the disciples and the crowds to pray and allow Himself to hear and know the will of the Father. He also said that we are to go into our "prayer closets" to pray. John 16:13 (BBE): "However, when he, the Spirit of true knowledge, has come, he will be your guide into all true knowledge: for his words will not come from himself, but whatever has come to his hearing, that he will say: and he will make clear to you the things to come."

If I don't prioritize prayer and read my Bible daily as a parent, how can I teach my children to do the same? When I know and value this truth, I can demonstrate and teach others. If I don't know and obey the Word of God, how will I know the convictions and voice of the Spirit of God, who is teaching me as a believer in Christ? The Holy Spirit inspired obedient men to write the Bible. The Bible is the Holy Spirit's language of communication with mankind. Second Peter 1:20–21 (ISV): "First of all, you must understand this: No prophecy in Scripture is a matter of one's own interpretation, because no prophecy ever originated through a human decision. Instead, men spoke from God as they were carried along by the Holy Spirit." Know what is written in the Bible, and you will recognize the voice of the Holy Spirit.

Every family is unique, and work schedules vary; however, I encourage the available parent to set aside a time each day to pray and read Bible stories with the children. Also read other confidence-building books with them about people who have done great things against all odds. This will help them dream to do great things and also pray for God's direction. When both parents are available, then the entire family can pray together, even if it's a few days or once a week. My husband, being a pediatrician, is often on call or working through the night. I decided from the beginning of our marriage to cover my husband and children daily in prayer, including taking on the responsibility of bringing the children to church. It is important to me that my children receive a godly upbringing. This also means that I make myself available to willingly serve in the church as an example to my children, since actions speak much louder than words.

I hug and bless the children in the morning and pray with them as I drive them to school. After school, upon returning home, I read a chapter or two of the Bible out loud as they are eating. We keep a Bible on our breakfast nook table as a reminder to read Scripture. Before bed, we read more Scripture, and we pray for each other. On Fridays and Sundays, especially when my husband is home in the evening, he joins us in reading Scripture and in prayer and thanksgiving to God for bringing us through the week, and then he blesses his family for the coming week.

Depending on the age of your children, read through the Bible together during the year. There are many Bible stories that cover every challenge we and our children will face in life. Our God is so faithful and loving and will work with us, no matter the circumstances, to get us where we need to be.

As we honor God and continue to allow the Holy Spirit to guide us through the Word of God, our minds are transformed, our faith increases, and our behavior changes for the better. We begin growing spiritually, speaking like Jesus, praying like Jesus, loving people like Jesus, trusting God like Jesus, acting like Jesus, and maturing in Christ, all to the glory of our heavenly Father. With the help of the Holy Spirit, we parents and guardians can train our children to love and respect God and other people the same way that Daniel and his friends did.

Additional Reflection Verses

1 Corinthians 2:10 (BBE): But God has given us the revelation of these things through his Spirit, for the Spirit makes search into all things, even the deep things of God.

1 Peter 4:14–16 (ERV): When people say bad things to you because you follow Christ, consider it a blessing. When that happens, it shows that God's Spirit, the Spirit of glory, is with you. You may suffer, but don't let it be because you murder, steal, make trouble, or try to control other people's lives. But if you suffer because you are a "Christ-follower," don't be ashamed. You should praise God for that name.

Ephesians 1:17 (ERV): I always pray to the great and glorious Father, the God of our Lord Jesus Christ. I pray that he will give you the Spirit, who will let you know truths about God and help you understand them, so that you will know him better.

Acts 2:4 (WEB): They were all filled with the Holy Spirit, and began to speak with other languages, as the Spirit gave them the ability to speak.

Romans 8:11 (BBE): But if the Spirit of him who made Jesus come again from the dead is in you, he who made Christ Jesus come again from the dead will in the same way, through his Spirit which is in you, give life to your bodies which now are under the power of death.

Chapter 4

Grieving the Holy Spirit

The Holy Spirit of God has sealed you in Jesus Christ until you experience your full salvation. So never grieve the Spirit of God or take for granted his holy influence in your life. Lay aside bitter words, temper tantrums, revenge, profanity, and insults. But instead be kind and affectionate toward one another. Has God graciously forgiven you? Then graciously forgive one another in the depths of Christ's love.
(EPHESIANS 4:30–32 TPT)

One of the problems we have in the church today is that many are blind and deaf to the guidance of the Holy Spirit because they don't reverently fear God or take the Bible seriously. They love the blessings but ignore the One who blesses. Many church-attending Christians, for example, seek psychics for advice before making decisions rather than pray, search the Scriptures, and seek godly counsel.

When I was a child in Kenya, I was introduced to horoscope readings, psychics, and palm readers and saw the utter devastation of my family and community due to these satanic practices. Idolatry will attract evil and chaos into the family like nothing else and hinder the godly training of children.

For the Holy Spirit to be grieved, it means He has feelings, which means He possesses a personality like us. The Bible says that in the beginning God created man in His Image. We have emotions because God has emotions. Like us, the Holy Spirit also feels pain, sadness, joy, etc. When we obey Scripture, it means we are following His guidance, so He rejoices. However, if we ignore Him because we are too busy and too distracted, He is saddened or grieved. Why is He grieved? He's grieved because sin destroys us and our relationship with God and others. The Holy Spirit desires to express the love and holiness of God to others through our speech and deeds. The Bible also talks about quenching the Spirit. Quenching points to putting out a fire. The Holy Spirit is the fire living in us. The Bible talks about taking on the shield of faith to quench the fiery darts of the enemy. A lack of faith or trust in God means a rejection of the Word of God and His Holy Spirit, which will lead to more sin and deception. Grieving and quenching the Holy Spirit will hinder godly character. Psalm 119:9 (ERV): "How can a young person live a pure life? By obeying your word."

We do not need to search for answers in the wrong places or from people who have no regard for the living God. The Bible warns us to keep away from psychics, fortune-tellers, mediums, and other similar individuals. Such individuals have what are known as familiar spirits, or snake spirits, which are lying, seducing, and deceiving spirits with the purpose of leading people away from trusting God solely. Isaiah 8:19–20 (*Voice*): "People might tell you to ask the fortune-tellers, consult the babbling astrologers, conjure the dead to tell the living what's to come, but shouldn't they ask their God? Go to God's teaching and His testimony *to guide your thoughts and behavior*! If any response disagrees with the word of God, then it's *muddling and wrong and* not the least bit illuminating."

Once an individual chooses to look for answers in other people, immoral experiences, or alcohol and drug abuse (including abuse of prescription drugs) rather than in the Word of God, through prayer, and from God-appointed shepherds, then the enemy gets the legal right to come into their life and wreak all kinds of havoc—uncleanness (defilement, corruption), fears, hopelessness, depressions, addictions, sicknesses, strife, oppressions, confusions, deceptions (including being used to lie and deceive others with various untruths), unexplained illnesses, destruction of relationships, immorality, premature death, and finally, eternal damnation. Leviticus 19:31 (KJV): "Regard not them that have familiar spirits, neither seek after wizards, to be defiled by them: I am the Lord your God."

Seeking counsel from psychics and fortune-tellers is idolatry because God is not the source of the information being given, Satan is. Idolatry causes the Lord to withdraw His hand of protection. Then Satan and his evil forces are able to invade an individual's life more freely, bringing in more deception and corruption. Sin brings on a curse, and when there is no repentance because of either ignorance or love of the sin, then negative consequences are the result.

God is love, full of mercy and grace. However, He is also holy, righteous, and just. His righteousness and justice demand punishment for sin. Satan knows this, so he tempts and deceives us to go ahead and sin knowing that God's law demands punishment for sin. Then he rushes to God to accuse and demand that we must pay for wrongdoing. The Bible calls him the accuser of the brethren.

For our sake and our children's sake, beware of books, websites (plus internet access through cell phones, watches, iPads, and other electronic devices), video games, television shows, movies, and music that promote, condone, or sympathize with what the Lord calls evil and abominable. Beware of spell-casting, horror, or vampire movies and books, as they release spirits of fear to oppress children. Beware of sensual, lewd movies and music, as they release spirits of perversion. Isaiah 5:20–21 (BBE): "Cursed are those who give the name of good to evil, and of evil to what is good: who make light dark, and dark light: who make bitter sweet, and sweet bitter! Cursed are those who seem wise to themselves, and who take pride in their knowledge!" For there you will find Satan at work leading into evil, brainwashing, deceiving, and teaching children to accept what is dangerous, harmful, and evil.

The great news is that God's love and mercy found a way long ago to punish all sin and restore our relationship with Him. He sent the Lord Jesus to take our punishment for sin by shedding His blood on the cross. When we repent, our heavenly Father forgives us and remembers the sin no more, washing us clean, as though we had not sinned, and restoring us to a right relationship with Him. By depending on the Holy Spirit and obeying the Bible, we receive what we need to lead successful lives that are considerate of others and that glorify God.

Additional Reflection Verses

Deuteronomy 18:10–14 (CJB): There must not be found among you anyone who makes his son or daughter pass through fire [that is sacrificing or murdering babies, included here is murdering unborn children—also known as abortions], a diviner [an observer of times through black magic], a soothsayer [fortune-teller, psychic, sign-reader, palm-reader, tea-leaf reader, augur], an enchanter [serpent charmer], a sorcerer [witch, wizard, warlock], a spell-caster [one who casts spells on others], a consulter of ghosts or spirits [a medium or consulter of familiar spirits, one who holds séances or spirit-communication meetings, an occultist or spiritualist], or a necromancer [one who seeks the dead or is involved with ancestral worship]. For whoever does these things is detestable to *Adonai*, and because of these abominations *Adonai* your God is driving them out ahead of you. You must be wholehearted with *Adonai* your God. For these nations, which you are about to dispossess, listen to soothsayers [fortune-tellers] and diviners; but you, *Adonai* your God does not allow you to do this.

Deuteronomy 18:15 (WEB): Yahweh your God will raise up to you a prophet from the midst of you, of your brothers, like me; to him you shall listen.

Galatians 5:19–21 (NKJV): Now the works of the flesh are evident, which are: adultery, fornication, uncleanness [all perversions including impure thoughts, pornography, prostitution, masturbation, pedophilia, incest, bestiality, practicing homosexuality], lewdness [indecency, lasciviousness—including all obscene speech], idolatry [including practicing yoga, any religion or ideology that denies and/or rejects Christ's divinity and lordship, crucifixion, death and resurrection], sorcery [all witchcraft, occultism and drug abuse], hatred [including racism, tribalism, misogyny], contentions [fighting], jealousies, outbursts of wrath, selfish ambitions [cut-throat mentality], dissensions [disputes], heresies [group rivalry, cliques, secret societies], envy, murders [including abortions], drunkenness, revelries [wild parties, orgies], and the like; of which I tell you beforehand, just as I also told *you* in time past, that those who practice such things will not inherit the kingdom of God.

Acts 19:19 (ESV): And a number of those who had practiced magic arts brought their books together and burned them in the sight of all. And they counted the value of them and found it came to fifty thousand pieces of silver.

Revelation 21:8 (KJV): But the fearful, and unbelieving, and the abominable, and murderers, and whoremongers, and sorcerers, and idolaters, and all liars, shall have their part in the lake which burneth with fire and brimstone: which is the second death.

Chapter 5

How My Experiences with Occult Practices Kept Me from Considering Others

I will put an end to your use of secret arts, and you will have no more readers of signs: And I will have your images and your pillars cut off from you; and you will no longer give worship to the work of your hands.
(MICAH 5:12-13 BBE)

My two siblings and I were born in Kenya to well-educated non-Christian parents. My father, a prominent and brilliant doctor, was a Muslim, while my mother, a respected and successful accountant, practiced Transcendental Meditation (TM). Though marketed in the United States and around the world as neutral and nonreligious, TM is deeply rooted in Hinduism—a pantheistic religion with millions of gods. The Bible is clear that there is only one holy and living God. Isaiah 46:9–10 (WEB): "Remember the former things of old: for I am God, and there is no other. I am God, and there is none like me. I declare the end from the beginning, and from ancient times things that are not yet done. I say: My counsel will stand, and I will do all that I please."

The Word of God is the manual for good manners, as it shows us how to truly consider others and glorify God in the process. Satan hates the Word of God because when we obey it, it draws us closer to a holy and good God, ushering in all kinds of blessings to our families. Disobeying the Word of God will bring curses, fears, insecurities, and destruction to our families. The purpose for this chapter is to use the Word of God to expose and dismantle deceptive reasonings, evil ideologies, and false philosophies that keep many bound in various satanic practices that, many times, they are not aware of. Second Corinthians 10:4–5 (TPT): "For although we live in the natural realm, we don't wage a military campaign employing human weapons, *using manipulation to achieve our aims*. Instead, our *spiritual* weapons are energized with divine power to effectively dismantle the defenses *behind which people hide*. We can demolish every deceptive fantasy that opposes God and break through every arrogant attitude that is raised up in defiance of the true knowledge of God. We capture, like prisoners of war, every thought and insist that it bow in obedience to the Anointed One." Christ tells us that from the beginning Satan has been a liar and a murderer. It is his very nature to lie and deceive. Satan has cunningly and successfully used numerous false doctrines to mislead, paralyze, cripple, sabotage, and destroy individuals, families, communities, and nations.

My father passed away when I was four years old. My mother worked hard to provide and give us a good education. Transcendental Meditation was introduced to my mother in the early eighties by her brother, after the trauma of my father's sudden, tragic death. The teachings of TM promised to help her "cope" with anxiety and stress. She embraced the new religion so much that it became her mad obsession as she sought for peace, greater mental ability, and a way to reach a more enlightened self. The Bible reveals that joy, peace, and comfort are not something we get from within ourselves, but from Jesus Christ. Indeed, He is the source of every good thing. Isaiah 9:6 (KJV): "For unto us a child is born, unto us a son is given: and the government shall be upon his shoulder: and his name shall be called Wonderful, Counsellor, The mighty God, The everlasting Father, The Prince of Peace."

Even when we were young, my mother would take us to the TM meetings in Nairobi, the capital city of Kenya, where we were taught yogic breathing and yogic postures while meditating and mentally repeating a mantra—a secret Hindu holy word—for fifteen to twenty minutes minimum, twice a day or more. The teachers said to help transcend to a "higher" status, we needed to focus our mental capacities on something like a lighted candle and nothing else, while mentally repeating the secret, holy word. The longer and the more often we meditated, the faster we would be facilitated to that "higher" divine consciousness, like Maharishi Mahesh Yogi, the founder.

Practicing Transcendental Meditation, the teachers taught, would cause us to use our brains more effectively, hence enhancing our lives. In fact, they said most people barely used 10 percent of their brain. With TM, they promised, we could greatly increase that percentage. The Bible reveals that meditating on and obeying the Word of God is what will bring success and prosperity to every area of our lives. Joshua 1:8 (ESV): "This Book of the Law shall not depart from your mouth, but you shall meditate on it day and night, so that you may be careful to do according to all that is written in it. For then you will make your way prosperous, and then you will have good success."

We were told that the mantra or holy word is secretly, uniquely, and individually selected by a TM teacher, or in our case, by the founder—Maharishi Mahesh Yogi himself. I found out years later that my sister and I had the same mantra, and anyone in the same age group had the same mantra too! Mantras are given according to age group and gender. I was about twelve years old when I received mine, and my brother ten. My sister had received her mantra as a teenager. The teachers said these mantras had no meaning. They were simply to help us focus. Really? Further research and study reveal that these mantras are abbreviated names of Hindu gods, which individuals are given to silently chant, then repeat mentally. How do I know this? My mantra was *inga*, which means to bow down to the household god of learning, music, speech, and the arts. How disturbing. So chanting or mentally repeating a mantra is worshiping a false god and yoking oneself to it. First Timothy 4:1–3 (NKJV): "Now the Spirit expressly says that in latter times some will depart from the faith, giving heed to deceiving spirits and doctrines of demons, speaking lies in hypocrisy, having their own conscience seared with a hot iron, forbidding to marry, *and commanding* to abstain from foods which God created to be received with thanksgiving by those who believe and know the truth." Regarding meaningless repetitions, the Scripture states in Matthew 6:7 (WEB), "In praying, don't use vain repetitions, as the Gentiles do; for they think that they will be heard for their much speaking."

The mantra given is never to be revealed by the learner to anyone, otherwise it will "lose" its healing and enhancing powers. The day my brother and I received our mantras, we were in a class of about twenty people. We were each given a headphone, both adults and children, and warned to keep our mantras secret; otherwise we would not reach our full potential, that untapped source of power within us, which would eventually bring world peace. After a period of silence, a man with an Indian accent spoke the secret word. From that day forward, we spent about twenty minutes silently chanting the mantra while seated in a yogic posture, with eyes closed, imagining a lit candle. In retrospect, after a TM session, I would feel a heaviness and mental fog of some sort, a burdening or yoking that I eventually just yielded to. The Bible reveals that there is only one way to God and that is through Christ Jesus. He is the Healer, the only Mediator to the Father, the only Truth, the only Way, and the only Light. Jesus said in John 10:9–10 (WEB), "I am the door. If anyone enters in by me, he will be saved, and will go in and go out, and will find pasture. The thief only comes to steal, kill, and destroy. I came that they may have life, and may have it abundantly."

Our family was baited with promises that we would be happier, brighter, more energetic, healthier, tranquil people through TM. What we ended up with was horrifying paranoia, deep insecurities, physical, emotional, and mental disturbances, deception and bondage, and destroyed relationships due to anger, unforgiveness, strife, and bitterness. Second Kings 17:15 (ISV): "They rejected the Lord's statutes, the covenant that he had made with their ancestors, and his warnings that he gave them. They pursued meaninglessness—and became meaningless themselves—as they followed the lifestyles of the nations that surrounded them, a practice that the Lord had warned them not to do."

The grounds of the TM center were impeccable—beautifully manicured lawns and shrubs, with the delightful aroma of blooming flowers all around. The place looked tranquil, relaxed, and blessed, yet it was hiding something evil. We can have good etiquette, but our heart can be far from good manners. Eventually negative emotions like hatred and rage will pour out. The facade of TM couldn't be kept up forever, and neither can a person with an evil heart consistently demonstrate love and kindness.

All the teachers spoke in soft voices and appeared to be so friendly, so wise, so peaceful, and so fulfilled. This all added to the deception that surely the TM teachers must know what is truly good for us. We were taught that TM was religiously neutral and that all people from all religions were welcome. In fact, under TM, they said, there would be peace among all religions if they followed the teachings of the founder, Maharishi Mahesh Yogi. We were taught pantheism: that God is simply a force or power that is in everything—people, trees, snakes, tables, etc.—so everything is divine, and we could even bow down to these things and call them "god." What? The Bible reveals that we cannot reach God within or by ourselves. In fact, we are separated from the Holy and Righteous God because of sin, and the only way to Him is by believing in Jesus Christ. It is by accepting Jesus as Lord and Savior that we receive forgiveness and are reconciled to a holy God. There is no peace, righteousness, or salvation without Jesus Christ. Romans 10:9–10 (WEB): "That if you will confess with your mouth that Jesus is Lord, and believe in your heart that God raised him from the dead, you will be saved. For with the heart, one believes unto righteousness; and with the mouth confession is made unto salvation."

The TM center often displayed pictures of the founder, Maharishi Mahesh Yogi, always with a glow behind and around his head. This reminds me of the Scripture in 2 Corinthians 11:13–15 (BBE): "For such men are false Apostles, workers of deceit, making themselves seem like Apostles of Christ. And it is no wonder; for even Satan himself is able to take the form of an angel of light. So it is no great thing if his servants make themselves seem to be servants of righteousness; whose end will be the reward of their works."

Maharishi was always dressed in Hindu priest attire—white sheet wrappings all over his body from shoulders to feet. He had a long beard and was always seated in a yogic posture and spoke in a calm voice with flowers and candles around him. He also smiled and giggled a lot. Again, appearances can be deceiving to what is underneath. The teachers at the center said that the flowers grew in his presence because he was at such peace and was one with "God" (that is the Hindu god Brahman) and that we, too, only through Transcendental Meditation, could eventually acquire the same "higher consciousness." The teachers also said that when Maharishi meditated, due to his "high" conscious status, his body did not remain on the ground but levitated or ascended in the air. We would be able to do the same in time. I remember seeing one of my uncle's attempting to levitate, but he was, in my observation, using a lot of energy to jump while seated in the yogic position. It was scary to watch and hear. Isaiah 48:22 (WEB): "'There is no peace,' says Yahweh, 'for the wicked.'"

There is also a great financial cost for joining and learning TM. In addition to the entry fee, during the initiation ceremony, we brought monetary gifts and other offerings like flowers and handkerchiefs, which were placed near the "glowing" picture of Maharishi's master-teacher, Guru Dev, who the teachers kept reminding us had himself reached a "higher" consciousness and was now one with "God" in the heavens. The picture where incense is burned and offerings are placed is an altar where prayers are offered by the teacher on behalf of the initiate. The teacher then performs what is called the *puja*, which is a long Hindu prayer yoking the initiate to various Hindu gods, including Maharishi's master Guru Dev, who is now considered a god, as he has reached oneness with "God." The *puja* (Hindu prayer) worships and praises many of the Hindu gods as sources of life, protection, peace, wisdom, and all other goodness. (The initiates do not understand the prayer unless they are Hindu themselves.) After the prayer, we were encouraged to bow down to the picture, then were guided into a room where we received our mantras.

The problem with all this is that we were unknowingly worshiping demonic forces and giving them the legal right to come into our lives and wreak havoc. The living God says in Exodus 20:2–6 (NKJV):

I *am* the Lord your God, who brought you out of the land of Egypt, out of the house of bondage. You shall have no other gods before Me. You shall not make for yourself a carved image—any likeness *of anything* that *is* in heaven above, or that *is* in the earth beneath, or that *is* in the water under the earth; you shall not bow down to them nor serve them. For I, the Lord your God, *am* a jealous God, visiting the iniquity of the fathers upon the children to the third and fourth *generations* of those who hate Me, but showing mercy to thousands, to those who love Me and keep My commandments.

Deeper teachings of TM promoted and conducted palm and horoscope readings and many other dark practices, including the drinking and eating of certain unclean things. My mother became so interested in these practices, especially the fortune-telling, that she took my brother and me to several palm-reading sessions.

I received a terrible shock several years later in downtown Nairobi, as I waited to catch a bus home, when I recognized one of the TM teachers, and he looked like a vagabond. He looked so terrible, so scary, I pretended not to recognize him. He gazed at me so intently, it felt like a harsh warning not to follow his ways.

Even if I had not accepted Christ then, I can confidently say now that God protected me, because I somehow knew that the reason this teacher had fallen into such a predicament was because of TM. After accepting Jesus Christ as my Lord and Savior a few years later, I came to understand just how evil and extremely dangerous practicing

Transcendental Meditation truly is. Ezekiel 13:18 (NLT): "This is what the Sovereign Lord says: What sorrow awaits you women who are ensnaring the souls of my people, young and old alike. You tie magic charms on their wrists and furnish them with magic veils. Do you think you can trap others without bringing destruction on yourselves?"

Going to fortune-tellers, psychics, mediums, witches, wizards, diviners, shamans, and others like these will open your life to all kinds of satanic torment and oppression. Let us look at an example of how a fortune-telling spirit operates, or as the Scripture puts it, how it misleads and deceives not only the psychic but many others as well. Acts 16:16–18 (BBE): "And when we were going to the place of prayer, we came across a girl with a spirit which gave knowledge of the future, whose masters made great profit from her power. She came after Paul and us, crying out and saying, These men are the servants of the Most High God, who are giving you news of the way of salvation. And this she did on a number of days. But Paul was greatly troubled and, turning, said to the spirit, I give you orders in the name of Jesus Christ, to come out of her. And it came out that very hour." The deception of a psychic spirit is that it appears as if it's praising and pointing people to God or coming from God, but it instead desires to draw people to itself as their source of comfort and guidance. It's a crafty, deceiving, seducing kind of spirit. See also that such a spirit is powerless in the presence of true followers of Christ, who know and depend on Christ as their source of comfort and guidance.

Attending an all girls' Catholic boarding high school protected me, to some extent, from the gripping, addictive nature of TM. Due to mandatory Mass, Christian religious education classes, and a busy, grueling course of study, I was unable to continue practicing Transcendental Meditation. I eventually lost complete interest, and even when I tried to practice TM, I would immediately fall asleep. Nevertheless, I continued to experience all kinds of negative consequences, such as terrifying nightmares in which I was being chased by scary beings, or dreams where I was falling from the sky, unable to stop. I felt helpless, hopeless, and powerless. Often, I would awaken screaming after falling off my bed. I had all kinds of fears and phobias—I'd dream spiders were going to bite me. I struggled with mental slowness and fogginess that prevented me from studying efficiently. I was paralyzed with insecurities, low self-esteem, and depression, which caused me to be very withdrawn and fearful of what others thought of me. I learned to be friendly, yet trusted no one and dreaded everyone.

I was severely bullied in school, and being somewhat numb to it, I didn't tell anyone, not even my mother or teachers, as though it were okay. It seemed like I expected to be mistreated, rejected, and unloved.

My mother, on the other hand, had it much worse, for she became more and more obsessed with TM to the point of paranoia. She became extremely fearful, reclusive, emotionally devoid, unforgiving, extremely bitter, and angry. My mother experienced terrible headaches that caused her to stop working in her forties. She became a totally different person—someone we could not recognize, like she was possessed. We lost our mother. Though my mom was alive, we felt as though we were orphans. My brother also experienced some of that paranoia and stopped practicing Transcendental Meditation for good.

Scripture reveals that God is so loving and kind to all His creation. Matthew 5:44–45 (WEB): "But I tell you, love your enemies, bless those who curse you, do good to those who hate you, and pray for those who mistreat you and persecute you, that you may be children of your Father who is in heaven. For he makes his sun to rise on the evil and the good, and sends rain on the just and the unjust." However, if we choose to continue sinning, hurting others, and rejecting Him, then curses come upon any disobedient individual, family, or nation. My mother's mental health deteriorated into a devastating downward spiral. I watched as my extended family fought among each other over my grandparents' land in such vicious ways, later even dragging each other through the highest court of the land. Rejecting the Lord by disobeying His Word will bring great tragedy and devastation to any family and nation.

In 2 Kings 10, it is revealed that God appointed and used the fearless general Jehu to execute judgment against the evil house of Ahab, Jezebel, and their sons, and to destroy the false Baal prophets and their horrible places of worship. Jehu obeyed God to a point. He failed to destroy the high places that had the golden calves that had been constructed by King Jeroboam when God tore ten tribes from the house of King Solomon.

We first hear about the golden calf abomination after the Israelites had just been delivered out of Egypt, having crossed the Red Sea on dry ground, been delivered from Pharaoh and his great army, and were now camped by Mount Sinai awaiting God's instructions. The calf idol had been erected under the high priest's, Aaron's, direction and supervision when Moses had been on the mountain. The worship of a golden calf is a symbol of looking back, a returning to past comforts, a slavery to iniquity, addictions, perversions—doing whatever one feels like doing irrespective of the hurts and devastation it causes others, especially children. It reveals a very stubborn and rebellious mindset, attitude, and behavior. As a result, there is no reverence, no patience, and no trust in the living God; instead, an "I am my own god, following my own truth" mentality takes deep root and spreads like wildfire, influencing others to follow suit.

When Jehu did not destroy the high places—the golden calves of Jeroboam—he was in fact exposing the condition of his heart. Despite the victories from the Lord, he loved his past evil sins and pleasures too much to care about following what God had instructed. We see from Scripture that the people of Israel paid a high price. Due to their idolatry and continued godlessness of their political leaders, they were continuously attacked and victoriously defeated by their enemies and even lost portions of the blessed land the Lord had given them. Second Kings 10:30–33 (WEB):

Yahweh said to Jehu, "Because you have done well in executing that which is right in my eyes, and have done to Ahab's house according to all that was in my heart, your descendants shall sit on the throne of Israel to the fourth generation." But Jehu took no heed to walk in the law of Yahweh, the God of Israel, with all his heart. He didn't depart from the sins of Jeroboam, with which he made Israel to sin. In those days Yahweh began to cut away parts of Israel; and Hazael struck them in all the borders of Israel; from the Jordan eastward, all the land of Gilead, the Gadites, and the Reubenites, and the Manassites, from Aroer, which is by the valley of the Arnon, even Gilead and Bashan.

We always lose if we ignore God and continue sinning and disobeying His Word. Sooner or later, punishment is the result.

After completing high school, with all the turmoil in my life and family, I began to have a desire and a curiosity about church and Christianity. I had felt a peace from learning the Lord's Prayer and receiving Christian religious instruction in school. I remember sharing with my brother my desire to start attending church. This did not happen in Kenya, but it happened a few months later when I moved to the United States and lived with my beloved sister, Rue.

In retrospect, I realize now that the Holy Spirit was calling me to Himself! Thank God for His love! Thank God for His mercy! Thank God for King Jesus! Thank God for His prayer warriors—the true bride of Christ. Here is what the living Lord has done for me: Jeremiah 15:19–21 (web):

Therefore Yahweh says, "If you return, then I will bring you again, that you may stand before me; and if you take out the precious from the vile, you shall be as my mouth: they shall return to you, but you shall not return to them. I will make you to this people a fortified bronze wall; and they shall fight against you, but they shall not prevail against you; for I am with you to save you and to deliver you, says Yahweh. I will deliver you out of the hand of the wicked, and I will redeem you out of the hand of the terrible."

Additional Reflection Verses

Deuteronomy 4:19 (*Voice*): And don't ever *become so corrupt that you* look up into the sky and see the sun, the moon, and the stars—as if each of them were a god—and be led astray to bow down to them and worship them, which the Eternal your God has given to all the people on earth.

2 Kings 23:24 (erv): Josiah destroyed the mediums, wizards, the house gods, the idols, and all the horrible things people worshiped in Judah and Jerusalem. He did this to obey the law written in the book that Hilkiah the priest found in the Lord's Temple.

Isaiah 44:6–8 (web): This is what Yahweh, the King of Israel, and his Redeemer, Yahweh of Armies, says: "I am the first, and I am the last; and besides me there is no God. Who is like me? Who will call, and will declare it, and set it in order for me, since I established the ancient people? Let them declare the things that are coming, and that will happen. Don't fear, neither be afraid. Haven't I declared it to you long ago, and shown it? You are my witnesses. Is there a God besides me? Indeed, there is not. I don't know any other Rock."

John 10:1 (NKJV): Most assuredly, I say to you, he who does not enter the sheepfold by the door, but climbs up some other way, the same is a thief and a robber.

Chapter 6

My Salvation Story: How Christ Taught Me to Consider Others

All we like sheep have gone astray. Everyone has turned to his own way; and Yahweh has laid on him the iniquity of us all.
(ISAIAH 53:6 WEB)

My older sister, Rue, gave her life to Christ while in high school in Kenya. Most of the high schools in Kenya are boarding schools, either all girls' or all boys' schools. Many of these boarding schools are situated long distances from where the students reside. This means that most children from the ages of twelve to eighteen years of age—their entire teenage years—are separated from their parents for long periods of time, coming home only for short breaks, then returning to school for months at a time. After Rue gave her life to

Christ, she experienced much persecution from the family because of her Christian faith. Thankfully, God gave her the grace and the strength to endure and persevere, and with much prayer she knew that the Holy Spirit would work on her lost family.

As the Lord would have it, after a few years Rue was accepted by an American university and was granted a student visa to study in the United States. I was eight years old at the time. Before Rue left, she led our six-year-old brother and me in the salvation prayer from Romans 10:9 (NKJV), which says, "That if you confess with your mouth the Lord Jesus and believe in your heart that God has raised Him from the dead, you will be saved." At that time, we did not understand what she was saying, as we did not know God or attend church. However, an unforgettable seed was planted in my heart. I still remember that day vividly as Rue sat on my bed between my brother and me, with me on her left and my brother on her right.

In 1995, ten years after my sister's departure to the US, I came to visit her. By that time Rue had married a wonderful Christian man. Her love for Christ never wavered all those years apart; rather, it continued to increase. The very first night I came to my sister's house, I was eager to show them the large book of horoscopes my mother had given me as a gift before I left Kenya. With great excitement I informed my sister and brother-in-law I could tell them their future. My sister responded without a hint of shock, disgust, or anger. Rather, in a gentle tone, she said we could discuss the matter later. I put the book away.

Years later my sister disclosed that her husband was concerned about me and my behavior, wondering who on earth they had let into their home. But she'd comforted him, saying that the Holy Spirit would take care of it. And that He did! What power we have through Christ our Lord if we just believe His Word and let the Holy Spirit change hearts! First Corinthians 13:4–6 (ESV):

"Love is patient and kind; love does not envy or boast; it is not arrogant or rude. It does not insist on its own way; it is not irritable or resentful; it does not rejoice at wrongdoing, but rejoices with the truth."

As the months passed, I observed what a family under the authority of Christ looked like. I saw and experienced the fruit of the Holy Spirit—the love, peace, and joy of Christ through my sister. I remember thinking and wondering why she wasn't insulting, threatening, arguing, or trying to somehow force me into being a Christian. Such disturbing thoughts caused me to pay more attention to her, and in time, my walls of defiance and rebellion crumbled. The years without Christ and the years in Transcendental Meditation had left me confused and suspicious about people's intentions. I was always ready to argue against Christianity and its Christians. The rejection I experienced as a child due to my mother's emotional turmoil had left me with such low self-esteem, yet I had no knowledge or understanding about my sad condition. At the same time, I had an air of arrogance and prejudice that I had acquired through TM, where I thought I was smarter, knew more, and was better than others because I had this secret holy word (mantra) that was unlocking greater mental ability.

As my thick and tall walls of ignorance, rebellion, and stubbornness crumbled, my curiosity increased for the God my sister revered. I daily observed her devotion and faithfulness to Christ through her thoughtful words; acts of kindness; and service to me, her family, and others. First Peter 2:15–16 (ESV): "For this is the will of God, that by doing good you should put to silence the ignorance of foolish people. Live as people who are free, not using your freedom as a cover-up for evil, but living as servants of God."

The church my sister and her family attend hold biweekly Bible study cell groups in their members' homes, depending on location of residence. Rue and her husband often hold such fellowship and prayer meetings in their home. They are such faithful, generous, and loving people, yet incredibly humble. It was at one of these meetings, in my sister's house, that I not only began to hear testimonies of the goodness of God and hear the prayers of His people, but I also began to care for the children by playing with them while the parents enjoyed Bible study and fellowship.

After observing Rue's godly character and love for Christ, it was easy to join her in attending church and hearing the gospel preached. It wasn't long after that when I knelt by my bedside one night, just like I had observed my sister doing, and called on her God to reveal Himself to me and help me know Him personally. I had witnessed a joyous, peaceful, happy life and wanted what my sister had through Christ. Romans 2:4 (WEB): "Or do you despise the riches of his goodness, forbearance, and patience, not knowing that the goodness of God leads you to repentance?" I was unable to resist God's love and call any longer. A life-changing miracle took place in my mind and heart that night, because when I arose the following morning, the first words out of my mouth were, "Of course Jesus is Lord and Savior!" I experienced a range of emotions that morning: I was in shock and amazed at my confident verbal confession that Christ Jesus is Lord, yet ashamed and disturbed that all along I had rebelled and ignored Him. I wondered how, coming from such an educated family, I had not been able to figure out the truth about Christ before.

I later found out that no one can come to know Christ through worldly or human reasoning; it is the work of the Holy Spirit that causes us to respond to God's love and grace in Christ Jesus. All the money, amazing works, good looks, great education, and high connections cannot deliver us from falsehood. With the help of the Holy Spirit, we must all come humbly before the cross to bow and confess that Jesus Christ is Lord and Savior. First Corinthians 1:18–20 (*Voice*):

For people who are stumbling toward ruin, the message of the cross is nothing but a tall tale for fools by a fool. But for those of us who are already experiencing the reality of being rescued *and made right,* it is nothing short of God's power. This is why the Scripture says: I will put an end to the wisdom of the *so-called* wise, and I will invalidate the insight of your *so-called* experts. *So now,* where is the philosopher? Where is the scholar? Where is the skilled debater, the best of your time? *Step up, if you dare.* Hasn't God made fools out of *those who count on* the wisdom of this *rebellious, broken* world?

That same day I gave my life to Christ, I felt convicted about my large book of horoscopes. I knew two things: it was evil, and I had to get rid of it. I tore up the book of horoscopes into little pieces and threw them into the trash. I was concerned that if I threw it away whole, someone might salvage it and read it, ending up in the devilish mess I had been in. I felt like heavy weights had fallen off my shoulders. A joy and a relief I had never experienced before came flooding into my life. The TM bondages that had been blocking my mind from receiving the Good News about Jesus had been demolished. It took the patient, non-quitting prayers of my sister, her husband, and church family to get me delivered from the grips of evil. John 12:40 (web): "He has blinded their eyes and he hardened their heart, lest they should see with their eyes, and perceive with their heart, and would turn, and I would heal them." It takes intercession against the forces of darkness for an individual to be released from the clutches of evil. Therefore, it is paramount that we, followers of Christ, fast and pray for all people.

Isaiah 58:6 (NKJV): "*Is* this not the fast that I have chosen: To loose the bonds of wickedness, To undo the heavy burdens, To let the oppressed go free, And that you break every yoke?"

Miracles happen when real followers of Christ allow the Holy Spirit to love through them. The love of God conquers difficult situations; it's active and always produces good fruit or good manners in us, demonstrating that we consider others. Christians do not need to be rude and harsh to unbelievers, vigorously trying to force the Word of God down their throats, because they know it is the Holy Spirit who changes hearts and transforms lives. We simply need to live the Word of God by His grace. Paul the apostle says in 1 Corinthians 3:6 (KJV), "I have planted, Apollos watered; but God gave the increase." We are vessels, instruments, servants who sometimes plant seeds, sometimes water. However, it is the Holy Spirit who causes the growth, the change, the transformation. Oh, how we need to humble ourselves, seek the Lord in prayer, turn away from our wicked ways, and trust God to bring change in our lives, our families, our churches, our cities, and our nations. Psalm 81:13–14 (WEB): "Oh that my people would listen to me, that Israel would walk in my ways! I would soon subdue their enemies, and turn my hand against their adversaries."

Coming to know Christ changed my life and set me on a path of righteous and successful living. Romans 12:1–2 (WEB): "Therefore I urge you, brothers, by the mercies of God, to present your bodies a living sacrifice, holy, acceptable to God, which is your spiritual service. Don't be conformed to this world, but be transformed by the renewing of your mind, so that you may prove what is the good, well-pleasing, and perfect will of God." Only God knows all He has saved me from: the wrong decisions I would have made over these past twenty years, the wrong relationships. I'm not sure I would even be alive today.

Soon after giving my life to Christ, I started serving in the children's church and choir ministries. As the children learned from the simple

Bible teachings and Christian videos, I learned along with them and grew more grounded in my Christian faith. I encourage every Christian believer to not only attend a Bible-believing church but to also serve in your local church. Be water baptized and start tithing and giving offerings too. Giving of one's time, skills, and energy by serving in the house of the Lord may appear to many as insignificant, but to God, who sees the motives of the heart, it means everything.

Serve God as a child. Serve Him as a teenager. Serve God as an adult. Serve Him while single. Serve God when married. Serve Him when you feel like it. Serve God when you don't feel like it. Serve Him when you're offended. Serve God when everything seems all right. Serve Him when you're in pain and when in joy. Serve Him in every season of life, for God is worthy. He is glorious. God is wonderful, for He gave His son Jesus as a ransom for us.

My son, Andrew, from a tender age of five, chose to serve as a junior usher. There are many other opportunities for children to serve. For example, in drama, praise dance, kids' choir, hospitality, and cleaning ministries. Serving the Lord is not something to be forced upon an individual. It is the work of the Holy Spirit in the child's life as the child is brought up God's way by being taught the Word of God. These ministries are wonderful opportunities to develop children's character and social skills.

Serving and giving are acts of righteousness that please the Lord greatly and bring great changes in our character and many other blessings in our lives. We are never more like God than when we are loving, giving, and blessing others. Christ said in John 3:16 (BBE): "For God had such love for the world that he gave his only Son, so that whoever has faith in him may not come to destruction but have eternal life." In other words, let us humble ourselves and love God with everything we've got. Christ gave His life for us. We are called to give Him our lives daily. It is impossible to outgive God. He is the

Creator and Possessor of the heavens and the earth. God owns it all. Deuteronomy 10:12–13 (BBE): "And now, Israel, what would the Lord your God have you do, but to go in the fear of the Lord your God, walking in all his ways and loving him and doing his pleasure with all your heart and all your soul, Doing the orders of the Lord and keeping his laws which I give you this day for your good?" We always win when we put God first.

My pastors, Pastor Stephen R. Hill and his wife, Pastor Emilia, teach of the importance of knowing and believing the Word of God with uncompromising trust in the Lord for wisdom and direction for every area of the believer's life. Under their authority, teaching, and leadership as my spiritual parents, the Bible has become the living manual for my life, a bright light in a very dark world. Hebrews 4:12–13 (WEB):

For the word of God is living and active, and sharper than any two-edged sword, piercing even to the dividing of soul and spirit, of both joints and marrow, and is able to discern the thoughts and intentions of the heart. There is no creature that is hidden from his sight, but all things are naked and laid open before the eyes of him to whom we must give an account.

Additional Reflection Verses

Acts 4:12 (BBE): And in no other is there salvation: for there is no other name under heaven, given among men, through which we may have salvation.

Acts 16:31 (BBE): And they said, Have faith in the Lord Jesus, and you and your family will have salvation.

2 Timothy 1:9 (BBE): Who gave us salvation, marking us out for his purpose, not on account of our works, but in the measure of his

purpose and his grace, which was given to us in Christ Jesus before times eternal.

Titus 2:11–14 (WEB): For the grace of God has appeared, bringing salvation to all men, instructing us to the intent that, denying ungodliness and worldly lusts, we would live soberly, righteously, and godly in this present world; looking for the blessed hope and appearing of the glory of our great God and Savior, Jesus Christ; who gave himself for us, that he might redeem us from all iniquity, and purify for himself a people for his own possession, zealous for good works.

Chapter 7

Imperfect Parents as Role Models

Are you weary, carrying a heavy burden? Then come to me. I will refresh your life, for I am your oasis. Simply join your life with mine. Learn my ways and you'll discover that I'm gentle, humble, easy to please. You will find refreshment and rest in me.
(MATTHEW 11:28–29 *Voice*)

In the book of Genesis, we are introduced to two characters named Abraham and Sarah. Though people of God, they were not perfect people or parents. As they walked with God, they made many mistakes along the way, yet God, in His great mercy and love, worked in and through them to birth the Jewish nation and, ultimately, the Christian faith. Abraham and Sarah deeply desired a child of their own but had been unable to conceive. After many years, when Sarah was way past childbearing age in her late eighties and Abraham in his late nineties, God performed a great miracle and gave them a son. With God, there is no such thing as an impossible situation. Our part is to trust and obey Him.

One of the flaws we see with Abraham is lying. Sarah was a strikingly beautiful woman, and when they traveled to Egypt to live there for a while, Abraham was afraid that he might get killed if people knew she was his wife. Sure enough, when the Egyptian officers saw Sarah, they were awed by her beauty. However, Abraham told them she was his sister. The officers told Pharaoh about her unusual beauty, and he immediately brought her into his harem for himself. Pharaoh was so pleased with Sarah that he blessed and enriched Abraham with expensive gifts, including many animals and male and female slaves. However, God was not pleased with what was happening to Sarah and afflicted Pharaoh and his household with terrible skin diseases so that Pharaoh would realize that Sarah was actually Abraham's wife. Outraged, he commanded them both to leave his kingdom.

Again, Abraham lied to everyone about Sarah not being his wife when they went to Gerar. King Abimelech of Gerar did the same thing as Pharaoh, and upon hearing the news of her unusual beauty, sent for her to join his harem. Once again, the Lord was displeased and afflicted the king's wife and secondary wives with barrenness, then warned the king in a dream that he would surely die if he touched Sarah and did not return her, because she was the wife of Abraham, a prophet. Like Pharaoh, King Abimelech was grieved with Abraham and scolded him for lying and deceiving him so badly. He returned Sarah and as commanded by the Lord, asked Abraham to pray for him that the Lord would forgive him and heal his household from barrenness. To be sure all was well, Abimelech enriched Abraham with many gifts of animals and slaves, plus a thousand silver pieces to make up for taking Sarah.

The Bible says we reap what we sow and that the sins of the parents pass on to the children. We see the generational curses of fear, lying and deceiving others passing on from Abraham to Isaac, for he too lied that his wife was his sister. Isaac's son Jacob disguised himself and lied to his father that he was Esau so as to receive the firstborn blessing. Jacob's sons in turn lied and deceived him when they said that their brother Joseph had been torn to pieces by a wild animal, when in fact they had sold him off into slavery. We see here that if generational curses are not dealt with the biblical way, they worsen and cause increasing havoc from one generation to the next. With this understanding and because there are many in my family that I continue to pray for, I have made a personal choice to continually answer altar calls for prayer to break generational curses until I see every member of my family saved.

When I look at those who came before me in my family bloodline, I see a lot of generational curses. Thank God for the cross, blood, and resurrection of Jesus. We can pray, repenting of our sins, the sins of our parents, and those who came before them and opened the door to evil and the power or influence of addictions, immorality, anger, abuse, neglect, abandonment, divorce, etc. We can pray that those curses will be broken off of our lives so that our children won't have to suffer and struggle with the same evil issues generation after generation.

There is a big difference in character between children raised "in the world" and children raised "in the Word of God." God speaks of Abraham saying in Genesis 18:19 (KJV): "For I know him, that he will command his children and his household after him, and they shall keep the way of the LORD, to do righteousness and justice; that the LORD may bring upon Abraham that which He has spoken of him." God knew Abraham. He knew that Abraham was obedient, faithful, and trustworthy because Abraham had believed Him and accepted the call to leave his own people and go to a place far away that he did not know. That took great courage and faith. God was familiar with Abraham's heart and that it truly belonged to Him. Abraham's response to God's love and plan was trust and obedience. The Lord saw that Abraham was serious and singled him out. He selected and chose Abraham for greatness—to become the father of many nations. Second Chronicles 16:9 (ERV): "The eyes of the Lord go around looking in all the earth for people who are faithful to him so that he can make them strong. Asa, you did a foolish thing. So from now on you will have wars."

The first thing we learn from Abraham is that he was called righteous because he believed and heeded the voice of the Lord. As parents, this is our first call of duty—to simply believe and obey what God says in His Word. Being righteous means being in right standing with God. Jesus said in John 10:14–15 (WEB): "I am the good shepherd. I know my own, and I'm known by my own; even as the Father knows me, and I know the Father. I lay down my life for the sheep." After salvation, it is our responsibility as followers of Christ to cultivate our relationship with the Lord we believe in through prayer and biblical meditation. As we do this, we become familiar with our Lord's Voice—with what is pleasing and not pleasing to Him. John 10:27 (WEB): "My sheep hear my voice, and I know them, and they follow me." All people who call themselves Christians or who attend church are not necessarily Christ's sheep . . . only those who are continuing to hear, listen, and follow Christ are His sheep.

Our children learn mostly from what they see demonstrated in the home. They see the real us. Children see if we are truly serious about our faith or if it is just an occasional thing. They see if we really believe what we say. Children see if we take our relationship with the Lord seriously. They see our attitudes, our reactions, and responses. Children see if we really believe in the Bible or not. They see if we are truly sorry for our mistakes and if we depend on God. Children hear how we speak and what we say. They see what we watch and what we spend most of our time doing. Children see and know what things are important to us, what things are not, and how we handle challenges in life. They see how we truly treat people—our spouses, our siblings, our neighbors, other believers, the police, our government officials, our bosses and coworkers—and hear how we really feel about them. And then, children mimic the same language, attitudes, reactions, responses, and behaviors in the home, in the neighborhood, at school, at church, at the playground, and everywhere else.

For God to bring about what He has promised us and our families, as described in Scripture, it is our responsibility as parents to command, instruct, guide, and train up our children to know and obey the Lord that they may follow the path of righteousness and justice and pass it on to their own children when their time comes. This does not happen automatically. To be able to train others in the way of the Lord means we need to know God's Word first. It means we must take time to read and study it, even if we do not understand it at first. It means we are to humbly ask the Holy Spirit for understanding and grace to obey and teach His Word to the children.

It is impossible to teach others something we do not know or obey. The adage that children are to do what parents say and not what they do is not only erroneous, it is deceptively evil. Deceptive to adults in that they believe the lie that no integrity is needed on their part and deceptive to children in that they believe they can live in any way provided they say and do what sounds "right" when others are looking. The truth is that children will follow what their parents or guardians do despite what the parents say. Therefore, it is imperative that we, as parents and guardians, submit ourselves to the Holy Spirit and the Word of God so that we may learn what is right and pleasing in God's sight to be able to demonstrate righteousness to our children.

Notice that Abraham, an imperfect man, a husband and father, a successful and prosperous rancher and businessman, a great war hero, the first Hebrew and great patriarch of the Jewish nation and New

Covenant believers, the head of his household, was also the priest of his home. He not only prayed with his family but also watched over them by teaching them to keep the way of the Lord, that is, to keep doing what was right and pleasing to the Lord. Abraham was a godly example to his wife and household, and they responded by submitting to him. God noticed this, was impressed, and drew close to Abraham and made him His special "advisor."

The Bible tells us that the Lord, with two of His angels and appearing as three men, visited Abraham to reveal to him God's plan to destroy the cities of Sodom and Gomorrah because their terrible wickedness had reached His ears. God—Creator and Judge of the entire universe—comes to "consult" with Abraham, seeking his thoughts and intercession on the matter! How could something so glorious like this happen? The King of the universe came down from heaven with the intent of avenging the evil done to the many victims of Sodom and Gomorrah, and decided, instead, to stop and seek the advice of one human being? And based on His conversation with Abraham, God then made a final decision regarding Sodom and Gomorrah.

Here is something else noteworthy to encourage us to obey God and to show us the godly impact we have on our families and the world: The Lord revealed to Abraham that the cries of the victims were so great and deafening that He had to come and see for Himself if it really was that terrible. Yet, we see that because of the righteousness of Abraham and the spiritual role model that he was to his family, his prayers and commitment to the Lord surpassed in importance the cries of the victims of injustice. There is just something about a heart that trusts and boasts about God to others that the Lord cannot resist.

Abraham teaches us that there are steps we can take to have life-changing encounters with God. First, we must place ourselves in position to hear and receive from God. This only occurs from an obedient and devoted life to Christ. Genesis 18:1 (NLT): "The LORD appeared again to Abraham near the oak grove belonging to Mamre. One day, Abraham was sitting at the entrance to his tent during the hottest part of the day." The significance of sitting at the entrance of the tent (home), in the heat of the day, was Abraham's readiness, openness, and willingness to meet and interact with anyone who needed him, including God. Abraham had placed himself in position for an encounter. He did not relegate or depend on Sarah, his wife, or a servant or child to sit at the entrance of the tent. They had their duties. Abraham's first duty was to seek God. He was the head of his household and took his spiritual responsibilities seriously. Sitting at the entryway of his home, Abraham could watch over his family's activities inside the tent and watch over the activities taking place outside. He was not distracted by worldly temptations or negligent, but focused and attentive to all the activities taking place in his home and with his household.

As parents and guardians, are we aware of what influences—good or bad—are coming into and out of our homes? Are we aware that there are evil spiritual forces eager to destroy our homes, marriages, children, and destiny? Are we vigilant in prayer over ourselves and our families? Do we care about what the Holy Spirit is saying to protect us from evil? Are we aware that He desires to talk to us about the great plans He has in store for us and our children? The more we are willing to know God's Word and obey it, the more accustomed and sensitive we will be to His voice and special visitations. Abraham could have been distracted by umpteen things, but he was not.

When the three men appeared, Abraham raised his eyes and saw them in front of him. He responded by running to them, paying them obeisance, and pleading with them to have a meal before continuing with their journey. They accepted. Abraham's discernment, mercy, thoughtfulness, kindness, and generosity are what etiquette and good manners are all about. This reminds us of what Paul, the great apostle and teacher of the faith, said in Hebrews 13:2 (*Voice*), "Don't forget to extend your hospitality to all—even to strangers—for *as you know,* some have unknowingly shown kindness to heavenly messengers in this way."

Abraham exemplified hospitality by giving his best to God. He hurried into the tent to tell Sarah to use three measures of the best flour, knead it, and prepare bread for the guests. The whole process of making and baking bread took time, yet Abraham was eager to get it done right, and the Lord was pleased and willing to wait. Using the best flour signifies giving our very best to guests and treating them with great dignity.

Abraham then ran to the herd and chose a fat calf to be prepared by a servant. Again, choosing a fat calf speaks of giving one's best to others. Abraham jumped at the opportunity to give God his very best. In many cultures, including my African culture and even Middle Eastern cultures, a calf is chosen and given a special fattening diet to make it tender and flavorful. The fattened calf is only slaughtered for special occasions and for important people. Not to mention the time and process of taking a live animal and transforming it into a cooked meal on the table. Remember that Abraham lived thousands of years ago, without all the industrial and high-tech advancements we enjoy today. It was a long and messy process. Yet the Lord was willing to wait. God is so compassionate and patient with us and so willing to work in and through us.

After the meal had been prepared, Abraham served the guests himself. He was a humble man and willing to take the initiative in serving God and others. While the men were enjoying the feast-offering, God released a great and awesome promise to Abraham, saying that by the same time the following year when He returned, Sarah, Abraham's wife, would have a son. When the Lord is pleased with us, He blesses us. Humbling ourselves to serve others is a great virtue. Psalm 69:32

(NLT): "The humble will see their God at work and be glad. Let all who seek God's help be encouraged."

Abraham's faithfulness affected his servants as well. Remember faithful servant Eliezer? Eliezer was entrusted with great wealth to travel a very long distance to seek a worthy bride for Isaac, Abraham's son. When he got to the gates of the city after the long journey, what did Eliezer do? He knelt and prayed to the God of Abraham for guidance in choosing the right wife for his master's son.

Eliezer, who was originally from Damascus, a pagan city in Syria, was focused, loyal, dependable, and obedient. What a great example by Eliezer that the church can learn from on how to honor our Lord and Savior, Jesus Christ. We could say that Eliezer became an extension of Abraham. When you saw Eliezer, you saw Abraham. Like Eliezer, like Abraham. Eliezer was all about his master's interests. Who taught Eliezer to trust and pray to the living God? From whom did Eliezer learn to be so loyal and obedient? Who taught him righteousness? Abraham did. What an incredible story that teaches us today, thousands and thousands of generations later, the great value of being a good role model to others by being obedient, humble, honest, morally upright, faithful, trustworthy, and most importantly, possessing a servant's heart even when we stumble in our roles as a guardians or parents. Abraham was an imperfect parent, just as parents of today are, yet when we choose to be faithful in service to God and teach our children, we will reap the same great rewards that Abraham reaped.

Additional Reflection Verses

1 John 1:8 (*Voice*): If we go around bragging, "We have no sin," then we are fooling ourselves and are strangers to the truth.

John 15:4–5 (WEB): Remain in me, and I in you. As the branch can't bear fruit by itself, unless it remains in the vine, so neither can you, unless you remain in me. I am the vine. You are the branches. He who remains in me, and I in him, the same bears much fruit, for apart from me you can do nothing.

Job 17:9 (NLT): The righteous keep moving forward, and those with clean hands become stronger and stronger.

Isaiah 41:13 (BBE) For I, the Lord your God, have taken your right hand in mine, saying to you, "Have no fear; I will be your helper."

Chapter 8
Guardians as Role Models

But the mercy of the Lord is eternal for his worshippers, and their children's children will see his righteousness; If they keep his agreement, and have his laws in mind to do them.
(PSALM 103:17-18 BBE)

My maternal grandparents were born during British colonial rule and, like many Kenyans, experienced brutal, horrifying oppression. They belonged to the Gikuyu (Ge-ko-yo) tribe, also known in Swahili as the Kikuyu (Kee-koo-yoo) tribe—the largest tribe in Kenya. The Kikuyus are Bantu-speaking agricultural people who live on the very fertile slopes of Mount Kenya. Mount Kenya is the second largest mountain in Africa. When British explorers first arrived in Kenya in the nineteenth century and saw the incredibly beautiful mountain, they asked for its name and were told "Kirinyaga" (Ke-re-nya-ga). However, unable to pronounce it correctly, they resolved to call it Mount Kenya instead. "Kirinyaga" means "crown of white patches," due to the snow on the mountain's peaks.

The Kikuyu tribe is divided into clans then subclans. My grandparents belonged to the Ambui (Am-boi) clan, and their sub-clan was Ambui wa Marigu (Am-boi wa Ma-ree-go), which literally means, "The people of the Ambui clan who plant bananas." I remember feasting on these super-sweet small yellow bananas on my grandparents' farm as a child, and I can tell you with all confidence, they are worth traveling to Kenya for.

Before the war broke out in 1952, between mostly Kikuyu young men and British forces, my grandparents lived on their own land, called a homestead. Traditionally, a Kikuyu homestead was comprised of several thatched houses, the family farmland, and barns for their livestock. As the war raged on, my grandparents, along with many other Kikuyu families, were stripped of all their possessions and forcibly evicted from their homesteads into heavily guarded village reserves. The British government was then able to allocate the vast pieces of fertile farmland to European settlers. The move was also a way for the British government to prevent Kikuyu families from supplying food to the freedom fighters in the Mount Kenya forests.

The formal education provided to natives was limited to a few years of primary school, just enough to be useful as cheap labor for the settlers and colonial government. As British rule became widespread, demanding more territory and more labor, war broke out, and a state of emergency was declared. The British military was deployed to hunt down insurgents and bomb their hiding places—the forests of Mount Kenya. My mother saw, as a child, bombers fly over her family's homestead.

Many native Kenyans, both men and women, especially the Kikuyus from the Kiambu (Kee-am-boo) area near Nairobi, were rounded up and thrown into concentration death camps, where they were tortured in unspeakable ways. Many were executed, and many others, especially Kikuyu women and children, were placed into heavily monitored villages. These villages resembled detention camps. They were surrounded with barbed wire and spiked, deep trenches and had watchtower guards, routine sirens, forced daily labor, and strictly enforced curfews. Anyone who did not return to the village on time was tied down and publicly flogged, many to their deaths.

The colonial government established village reserves that were crowded on unfarmable land, forcing many Africans to seek work on European farms and businesses. The British government further oppressed the people by imposing hut and poll taxes that forced many more Africans to work for settlers. Others moved to the cities for work as cooks, cleaners, guards, gardeners, and drivers. The colonists cunningly supported tribalism by ganging tribe against tribe to prevent mobilization of Kenyans against the government. Certain tribes were primarily used as home guards to spy upon other tribes, breeding resentment that has continued to this day. Since coffee and tea production were profitable, Kenyans were forbidden to obtain licenses to grow them. This resulted in many native Africans working as squatters to harvest colonial coffee and tea. They also worked in labor-intensive, very low-paying jobs like clearing forests, constructing railroads, and building offices.

In 1919 an identification system called the *kipande* (kee-pan-day) was implemented for Africans only. It was a colonist's tool of oppression to control forced cheap labor. All male Africans who looked like they were adults had to register with the colonial government and were issued a *kipande*—a small red book with their name, age, tribe, employment history, employer, and wage. The little red book was placed in a small metal box and worn, at all times, around the African's neck. Many times, evil employers would write unpleasant comments to prevent employment elsewhere. Or if native laborers absconded from work, the British police or African Home Guard would easily apprehend and forcefully return them to their employers.

Upon request by any British individual, the *kipande* had to be produced or the native risked grave punishment or imprisonment. Any disobedience by the African, proven or alleged, to any British law was met with harsh, injurious punishment, often culminating in fatalities. Psalm 10:13–14 (BBE): "Why has the evil-doer a low opinion of God, saying in his heart, You will not make search for it? You have seen it; for your eyes are on sorrow and grief, to take it into your hand: the poor man puts his faith in you; you have been the helper of the child who has no father." God considered the grief of the native Kenyans and eventually the *kipande* system was abolished, and in 1963 Kenya gained its independence.

Colonialism brought many oppressive evils, but despite the terrifying experiences for many decades, my maternal grandparents were some of the happiest people I knew. Not once did I hear them complain. Not once did I hear them express anger or hatred or vengeance toward those who caused them such pain, sorrow, and hardship. Nothing and no one were going to hold them back. My grandparents left us a great inheritance of their hard work and sweat: their thirty-acre farm, but much more importantly, they left us a legacy of love, hope, faith, endurance, hard work, and resilience. Their wishes were that the farm was not to be divided; instead, it was to be shared and enjoyed by all the grandchildren. And so the adage in Proverbs 13:22 (NLT) stands true, that "good people leave an inheritance to their grandchildren, but the sinner's wealth passes to the godly."

During both world wars, more land resources, higher taxation, and more forced human labor were demanded of the African native population. Kenya became a British military base against the Germans, and countless numbers of Kenyans were forced to fight as soldiers and sacrifice their lives. The tide did turn in favor, however, for many African countries after World War II, as the British and other European powers were financially devastated and unable to hold on so strongly to their colonies. Despite attempts by European imperialists to cover up their crimes against humanity in Africa, reports and evidence of these crimes kept increasing and circulating. Independence was also precipitated by the rise of African nationalism. Subject people had seen India granted its independence from the British in 1947. In addition, African soldiers returning home from war were not compensated for their sacrifices like the British soldiers, who were rewarded with much land and financial support. Africans hoped and desired to be free from foreign domination and racial discrimination, giving rise to African advocacy, political unions, and freedom-fighting militant groups like the Kenya Land and Freedom Army, widely known as the Mau.

The Mau Mau were mainly from the Kikuyu tribe. The fighters were young men and women. Many of the male Mau Mau, especially the leaders, were former soldiers who fought side by side with their European counterparts in the first and second world wars. These incredibly brave men and women, farmers with little or no formal education, were methodical and deadly, operating from the forests of Mount Kenya and the Aberdare mountainous regions. To the surprise and utter frustration of the British forces, these peasant farmers often evaded capture in forests and high caves, while conducting an uprising that lasted eight years, from 1952 to 1960. Unfortunately, tens of thousands of native Kenyans lost their lives, both insurgents and loyalists to the British. It was a terrible and bloody war. The Mau Mau fighters were outgunned yet fought with great resolve. They fought against a much more powerful, much better equipped, ruthless British military force and endured heavy losses. They lost the battle militarily but won the war politically, for three years later in 1963, Kenya received its independence.

The independence of African nations in the 1950s and '60s did not just happen. Pastor Stephen R. Hill says that nothing happens without prayer, for indeed the Lord had a plan for Kenya. He sent His apostles, prophets, evangelists, pastors, and teachers as missionaries to train Kenyans in teacher-training colleges. Many Kenyans were praying for a peaceful hand over of government. Surrounding newly independent African nations had not done so well; some had sunk into bloody civil war, while others became socialist-communist.

Great Bible teachers like Derek Prince were in Kenya before its independence, teaching and training young Kenyans. In one of his many great books, *Shaping History through Prayer and Fasting*, he mentions that in August of 1960, when he was ministering at a Christian convention of two hundred in western Kenya, the Holy Spirit came upon them powerfully, leading them in a two-hour spontaneous worship and prayer session. As they were praying, Derek Prince felt the conviction of the Holy Spirit to tell the young Kenyan teachers and students to pray for the future of their country. While praying, Derek Prince's interpreter, Wilson Mamboleo, received a vision in which he saw a red horse with a black man on it riding fiercely from the east toward Kenya. There were other red horses behind it, also fierce. As the participants continued in prayer, Wilson saw the red horses turn away from Kenya and go toward the north. The fulfillment of this vision came to pass within a few years. The book continues to recount that in 1964, a communist Ugandan individual having been trained under Castro in Cuba led a coup that overthrew the Zanzibar and Tanzanian governments, then attempted to do the same in Kenya. By the tactful actions of Kenya's first president, Mzee Jomo Kenyatta, he enlisted the help of the British military and squashed the communist attempt. Kenya has been a sort of Bible belt over the years, whereby Christians and Christian organizations have enjoyed the freedom to spread the gospel. While surrounding nations have suffered civil war and unstable political atmospheres, Kenya has continued to enjoy political stability to this day.

Nothing happens without prayer.

Leading up to and after Kenya's independence in 1963, the Kenyan government began to reinstate some of the lost lands to native Kenyans, something that is still going on today due to tribal land disputes. My grandparents were some of those who received land in the late fifties, and it was upon this land that they started to rebuild their lives. Deuteronomy 30:3 (*Voice*): "Then He will have mercy on you and bring you back from captivity. He'll gather you from all the peoples you've been scattered among."

My grandparents owned a large farm in a rural town called Murinduko (Mo-ren-do-ko), located in Kirinyaga County. My grandparents drank what they fetched and ate what they harvested and reared. Guka (goo-ka)—name for "grandfather" in Kikuyu—single handedly cleared their vast farmland of deep roots, thick bushy vegetation, and trees, armed with just a *panga* (machete) in hand, even ridding the land of cobras that had on many occasions almost blinded him. He subdued the land, making it conducive for farming and living. Cucu (sho-sho)—name for "grandmother" in Kikuyu—was a heroine in her own right. My mother often recounted a story of how Cucu overpowered a stubborn bull by bringing it to the ground!

Guka had a vast knowledge of the medicinal qualities of plants and would often remedy our ailments naturally. Even when my grandparents were well into their nineties, they still lived on their farm. They were strong, keen of mind, and had no experience of tooth decay or tooth loss their entire lives. Some of my fondest childhood memories were that of visiting Guka and Cucu and being led to their mango trees to pick out the sweetest, juiciest, largest, most delicious mangoes I have ever eaten. The rural air was always so fresh and clean, like nothing I have ever smelt before or again. The sound of streaming waters and the sound of chirping birds so unforgettable, Hollywood could not replicate. Job 12:7–10 (WEB): "But ask the animals, now, and they shall teach you; the birds of the sky, and they shall tell you.

Or speak to the earth, and it shall teach you. The fish of the sea shall declare to you. Who doesn't know that in all these, Yahweh's hand has done this, in whose hand is the life of every living thing, and the breath of all mankind?"

My grandparents also had a milling business where they would ground dried corn, millet, sorghum, and beans for sale. Their customers were their neighbors. Weekends and holidays were such special times for our family as we would gather with other family members at our grandparents' farm. My grandparents taught my siblings and me the value of hard work and being tenacious, of forgiveness and healing, of showing respect and being responsible, of possessing good character and being consistent through good and rough times. Guka and Cucu were people of action and people of their word. What they said they did. They loved their grandchildren so much and often blessed us with various gifts for good grades.

My sister, Rue, often shares wonderful memories of Cucu as a prayer warrior. She would wake up daily at 5:00 a.m. to pray earnestly for hours for each of her children and grandchildren by name. Rue lived with our grandparents for the first eight years of her life and was deeply influenced by Cucu's godly example. My sister recounts that whenever she was sick, Grandmother, in her sixties then, would carry her on her back and walk for miles, even in the rain, without shoes, up hills and down valleys, looking for a health clinic. I remember many times seeing Cucu dancing and singing praise songs to God unabashedly. I am convinced we are believers in Christ today because of her prayers and example. James 5:16 (WEB): "Confess your offenses to one another, and pray for one another, that you may be healed. The insistent prayer of a righteous person is powerfully effective." I am convinced we love and value our families deeply because of Cucu's great labors of love, strength, tenacity, and many sacrifices for the entire family. She laid down her life for us. I am convinced we inherited Cucu's passion for intercession, for life and, of course, for dance too!

Additional Reflection Verses

Isaiah 46:4 (BBE): Even when you are old I will be the same, and when you are grey-haired I will take care of you: I will still be responsible for what I made; yes, I will take you and keep you safe.

Proverbs 17:6 (ISV): Grandchildren are the crown of the aged, and the pride of children is their parents.

2 Timothy 1:5 (WEB): Having been reminded of the sincere faith that is in you; which lived first in your grandmother Lois, and your mother Eunice, and, I am persuaded, in you also.

Chapter 9

The Lord's Sheep

I am the good shepherd. I know my own, and I'm known by my own; even as the Father knows me, and I know the Father. I lay down my life for the sheep.
(JOHN 10:14–15 NLT)

I grew up hearing lots of intriguing stories about animals from my mother, grandparents, other relatives, teachers, and friends. Africans are social people and love to share stories with their children. In fact, that is the way history and good manners are taught in my Kenyan culture. I remember one such fascinating story about a wolf that disguised itself in sheep's skin and thought it could get away with it . . .

A wolf had gone hungry for some time. He searched and searched for prey to no avail. One morning, however, he awoke to some familiar sounds. To his great delight, they were sounds of bleating sheep—his favorite cuisine! However, he knew that where there were sheep, there were vigilant and dangerous shepherds who would not hesitate to kill him. Sure enough, it wasn't long before he heard the voice of the shepherds leading their sheep on.

Time and time again, the wolf tried to ambush, isolate, or lure a sheep or their lamb to their death, but they bleated so loud that the shepherds would descend upon him with their rods, called *rungus*, and at such lightning speed that he had almost lost his life on a number of occasions! What would he do? So one day in great distress, an idea popped up in his mind. He thought, *I know! I'll disguise myself as a sheep, sneak in with the sheep, pretend I'm a vegetarian. Then after I've won everyone's trust, I'll lead some of the sheep to their slaughter.* The wolf was so pleased with himself and his plans that he forgot about his hunger pains that night and slept like a well-fed baby.

The next morning, he arose with a new spring in his stride. He did not bother to even look at the sheep grazing nearby; instead, he ventured out to look for some flayed sheep's skin. The wolf found some and quickly disguised himself with it. This time, as he stepped out of the bushes to join the sheep, not one of them bleated. The sheep thought he was one of them. The wolf laughed to himself, amazed and relieved. Some even huddled next to him for companionship and warmth.

Soon, the ewes were allowing their lambs to follow him around. It wasn't long before he began to lead some of the lambs away to eat them, then quickly return to the flock. After a few weeks, he was the fattest "sheep" in the fold.

But one day, everything went wrong because the shepherds had been noticing that some of the sheep were sad and were not eating because their lambs had gone missing. That night, as the shepherds were herding the sheep into their pens, they decided to carefully examine each one as it entered through the gate, and, alas, there was the fat wolf! Without delay, they clubbed the wolf to death and burned its carcass to ashes. After that, and with the tenderness and comfort of the shepherds, the sheep were healed of their sorrow and loss and had many more lambs, living happily ever after.

So what are the morals of this story? Evil people eventually come to harm through their own deceit. What is done in secret will come to light. Those who hurt others will be hurt beyond remedy. Stay teachable, correctable, humble, and respectful.

It's interesting that we, the people of God, are called sheep. Sheep do not survive well on their own, especially after long periods of time. In fact, without protection and guidance, they have been known to fall over cliffs to their demise while eagerly following the dominant sheep. They are also easy prey to human thieves and dangerous predators such as wolves, foxes, bears, and lions. Following the example and instructions of antichrist leaders— also called wolves in sheep's clothing and who masquerade as individuals of light—have caused many to lose sight of the real Savior and Redeemer, Jesus Christ, and His intended purpose for their lives. First John 2:22–25 (NLT):

And who is a liar? Anyone who says that Jesus is not the Christ. Anyone who denies the Father and the Son is an antichrist. Anyone who denies the Son doesn't have the Father, either. But anyone who acknowledges the Son has the Father also. So you must remain faithful to what you have been taught from the beginning. If you do, you will remain in fellowship with the Son and with the Father. And in this fellowship we enjoy the eternal life he promised us.

Sheep need a shepherd to care for them, to yearly shear their wool and to provide medical remedies for injuries, diseases, worms, and parasites. Sheep need good shelter. They need a guide to lead them to safe pastures to graze and to find calm waters to quench their thirst. They are gregarious and group together when grazing or in the face of danger. Sheep follow other sheep they know because of the desire to stick together for protection. They also follow people they know, like those who feed them. In the same way, all human beings, whether they know it or not, desperately need a good and loving Shepherd—Jesus Christ.

The Lord has provided earthly shepherds to guide us through each stage of life, starting with godly parents and guardians, then ordained pastors who are after His heart. Today, many find it difficult or offensive to submit to authority because of disappointing experiences or because of what others say or because of their own pride and rebellion. However, submitting to God's appointed authority, such as parents and godly church leaders, provides a covering of spiritual protection, instruction, guidance, and success.

We need each other. We all need love and support. We also need encouragement, discipline, and wise counsel. Humbling ourselves and submitting to godly parents and church leaders will cause us to learn from them, gaining valuable knowledge, wisdom, and understanding to avoid making wrong choices and decisions. We learn that life is not about us. It's about letting God fulfill His purpose through us so that others may also come to know His Son, Jesus, and receive the same help we have received. Mark 16:20 (KJV): "And they went forth, and preached every where, the Lord working with them, and confirming the word with signs following. Amen."

It is sin, however, to accept and follow the example of evil, unrepentant leaders bent on disobeying the Word of God and leading others astray. Some leaders accept that they sin and mistreat others, but refuse to change. Justifying their bad behavior, they resolve to blame their parents, spouses, experiences, tradition, or culture. Jesus, responding to some Pharisees and teachers of religious law, says in Mark 7:9–13 (NLT):

Then he said, "You skillfully sidestep God's law in order to hold on to your own tradition. For instance, Moses gave you this law from God: 'Honor your father and mother,' and 'Anyone who speaks disrespectfully of father or mother must be put to death.' But you say it is all right for people to say to their parents, 'Sorry, I can't help you. For I have vowed to give to God what I would have given to you.' In this way, you let them disregard their needy parents. And so you cancel the word of God in order to hand down your own tradition. And this is only one example among many others."

Our first love is Christ. Our first duty, our total devotion, is to Christ, our Lord and Savior. Our call is to obey His Word, not a person's opinion or evil desires. Matthew 15:13–14 (ESV): "[Jesus] answered, 'Every plant that my heavenly Father has not planted will be rooted up. Let them alone; they are blind guides. And if the blind lead the blind, both will fall into a pit.'" For as long as appointed authority is holding fast to the Lord, we follow suit. The fact is, in the end, every one of us will have to give an account to God alone. This is one of the reasons why we are called to keep studying the Bible, to know what it says, and to keep asking the Holy Spirit for wisdom. We have no excuse. Second Timothy 3:16–17 (NLT): "All Scripture is inspired by God and is useful to teach us what is true and to make us realize what is wrong in our lives. It corrects us when we are wrong and teaches us to do what is right. God uses it to prepare and equip his people to do every good work."

Christ is our example. He submitted to our heavenly Father in all things. Christ said in John 6:38 (KJV), "For I came down from heaven, not to do mine own will, but the will of him that sent me." It is Christ's will that we all learn to be obedient and submit to Him by loving, encouraging, forgiving, and respecting each other. There is divine order for success in the believer's life. The church is called to submit to Christ. Husbands and wives are called to submit to God, then to each other. Children are called to submit to their parents. The people of God are called to submit to God by submitting to their pastors and other obedient church leaders, who are also submitted to the pastors. Hebrews 13:17 (WEB): "Obey your leaders and submit to them, for they watch on behalf of your souls, as those who will give account, that they may do this with joy, and not with groaning, for that would be unprofitable for you."

Employees are called to submit to their employers or bosses. Citizens are called to submit to government officials, which means respecting and praying for them and obeying the law. Romans 13:1–3 (NLT):

Everyone must submit to governing authorities. For all authority comes from God, and those in positions of authority have been placed there by God. So anyone who rebels against authority is rebelling against what God has instituted, and they will be punished. For the authorities do not strike fear in people who are doing right, but in those who are doing wrong. Would you like to live without fear of the authorities? Do what is right, and they will honor you.

There is protocol that dictates the proper strategy to defend just laws or to fight against oppressive ones. When the people of God trust Him and live obedient lives with persistent prayer, miracles happen, for justice is from the Lord. Proverbs 29:26 (WEB): "Many seek the ruler's favor, but a man's justice comes from Yahweh." Wicked leaders invite God's judgment upon them, sooner or later. Proverbs 28:16 (*Voice*): "A leader who lacks intelligence cruelly oppresses the people, but one who hates corruption will *prosper and* live a long life."

Learning to submit to God is a humbling and often long process that takes place under God's appointed authority, and the very reason we are called to stay planted in a Bible-believing church. If we are truly devoted to Christ and desire to fulfill divine purpose, we will trust Him as we go through a process of character change. Proverbs 25:4 (ERV): "Remove the worthless things from silver to make it pure, and a worker can make something beautiful." If we are stubborn, unruly, and unwilling, we end up stuck in a wilderness, going around a mountain like the Israelites did after being delivered from Egypt, for as long as the Holy Spirit deems fit.

Through the seasons of testing, we are stretched, and in our pain, we learn to obey, trust, and depend on the Lord alone. We discover how to use and develop our gifts, talents, and skills to serve God by serving others. Christ becomes the center of our world and we live to adore, worship, and serve Him. We are not baby Christians any longer, but spiritually mature and able to eat the meat of the holy Word of God. Like David, we become people after God's heart, eager to do His will. We grow from just being a part of a church (believers in Christ who may or may not be totally devoted to Him) to be the bride of Christ. A religious teacher asked Jesus what the most important commandment is. Mark 12:29–31 (NLT): "Jesus replied, 'The most important commandment is this: "Listen, O Israel! The Lord our God is the one and only Lord. And you must love the Lord your God with all your heart, all your soul, all your mind, and all your strength." The second is equally important: "Love your neighbor as yourself." No other commandment is greater than these.'"

When we as parents honor our own parents and submit to God-appointed leaders, it is a form of worship unto the Lord that brings glory and honor to Christ. We reap what we sow. So when our children observe their parents being respectful to the grandparents, they will imitate that same behavior. King David is a great example of someone who understood that obeying God and submitting to God-appointed authority go hand in hand, resulting in promotion. He submitted to his father by tending to the family sheep and goats.

David continued to submit and honor his father even when he was not counted worthy to meet the prophet Samuel when he visited their home. He remained humble even when he was not invited to partake in the sacrifice-offering to the Lord. David remained humble and continued to serve his father even after being anointed king of Israel by Samuel. His humility resulted in promotion after promotion, yet it did not go to his head. As a young teenager, he served King Saul as a harpist and continued to serve his father, Jesse, too. David would go back and forth as needed to perform his shepherd duties at home, since he was not in the military like his brothers.

God brought David through a long, painful process from the humble beginnings of watching over his father's sheep and goats to watching over God's people as shepherd and king. As he watched over his family's sheep, he learned important lessons about trusting and fearing God, for example, when he rescued the animals from a bear and lion. The difficulties with King Saul also helped develop David's character and dependence on God. David is remembered to this day as the great praise-dancer and worshiper whose heart was after God; as the mighty and fearless warrior of Israel; as the great intercessor, king, organizer, rescuer, builder, and protector of Israel; and as the great psalmist, having written the majority of the Psalms. Psalm 78:70–72 (web): "He also chose David his servant, and took him from the sheepfolds; from following the ewes that have their young, he brought him to be the shepherd of Jacob, his people, and Israel, his inheritance. So he was their shepherd according to the integrity of his heart, and guided them by the skillfulness of his hands."

Did you know that sheep have a four-compartment or four-chambered stomach? Each chamber serves a specific purpose in the digestion and extraction of nutrients, which means that sheep digest their food multiple times to extract the maximum amount of nutrients from the food they eat. Like sheep with their food, we—the people of God—are called to "graze" on the Word of God. We are called to feast on it while "standing," and to ponder on it while "sitting down resting." We are called to meditate on the Word of God daily and repeatedly through the day and night, through the week, through the months, and through each year of life. We are called to think about it, delight in it, believe it, and confess it. Jeremiah 15:16 (ESV): "Your words were found, and I ate them, and your words became to me a joy and the delight of my heart, for I am called by your name, O Lord, God of hosts."

We are called to declare the Word of God into our atmosphere, causing it to change. We are called to teach it. We are also called to share Scripture with others, bringing God's change, salvation, healing, and purpose in the lives of those around us. We are called to pray the Word of God, humbly asking the Holy Spirit, our Teacher, for clarity, understanding, and revelation. As we continue in the Word of God, our soul, which consists of the mind (thoughts), heart (emotions), and will (decisions), continues to be transformed, conforming us to Christ's will. We begin to have understanding, discernment, and clarity on what is truly right and what is truly wrong. We begin to understand and desire what is pleasing to the Lord. We begin to have holy and healthy desires rather than selfish ones. As understanding increases, the fear and reverence of God increases, resulting in humility and obedience. As the fear of God increases, so does the wisdom of God working wonders in all areas of life. Proverbs 3:15–18 (WEB): "She is more precious than rubies. None of the things you can desire are to be compared to her. Length of days is in her right hand. In her left hand are riches and honor. Her ways are ways of pleasantness. All her paths are peace. She is a tree of life to those who lay hold of her. Happy is everyone who retains her."

Rejecting and disobeying the Word of God will only bring a curse that leads to great deception and, eventually, eternal damnation. Christ leaves a warning that bids us to take heed. In John 12:48 (NKJV): Jesus said, "He who rejects Me, and does not receive My words, has that which judges him—the word that I have spoken will judge him in the last day." Christ Jesus restores, and He redeems, as revealed in Luke 15:3–7 in the parable of the lost sheep. He is the Good Shepherd that seeks out the lost sheep. When Christ finds the sheep, He carries it on His shoulders and restores it to the rest of the family of sheep already under His care. The carrying of sheep on Christ's shoulders is significant, as it illustrates God's great love, patience, tender mercies, and compassion for us.

Additional Reflection Verses

Matthew 10:16 (WEB): Behold, I send you out as sheep among wolves. Therefore be wise as serpents, and harmless as doves.

Ezekiel 34:16 (ERV): I will search for the lost sheep. I will bring back the sheep that were scattered and put bandages on the sheep that were hurt. I will make the weak sheep strong, but I will destroy the fat and powerful shepherds. I will feed them the punishment they deserve.

Matthew 18:12–14 (WEB): What do you think? If a man has one hundred sheep, and one of them goes astray, doesn't he leave the ninety-nine, go to the mountains, and seek that which has gone astray? If he finds it, most certainly I tell you, he rejoices over it more than over the ninety-nine which have not gone astray. Even so it is not the will of your Father who is in heaven that one of these little ones should perish.

Chapter 10

Meeting and Greeting Etiquette

Biblical Foundation
*And let us continue to consider how to motivate one another
to love and good deeds, not neglecting to meet together,
as is the habit of some, but encouraging one another even
more as you see the day of the Lord coming nearer.*
(Hebrews 10:24–25 ISV)

We are commanded to meet together, and when we do it correctly, the results are that we motivate and encourage each other. "Meeting and greeting" is a great witness of Christ's love to others. Christ is our greatest example. He is called the friend of sinners. In Luke 19 we are introduced to a man by the name of Zacchaeus, who was hated by his own people because he was a tax collector. He heard that Jesus was coming by and decided he wanted to see Him. There was a large crowd that wanted to see Jesus too, and because Zacchaeus was short in stature, he climbed a sycamore tree. It so happened that Jesus came near the tree, looked up, and saw him. Without hesitation and with great joy, the Lord called Zacchaeus to quickly descend because He was going to stay at his house. The Bible says that Zacchaeus was overjoyed and quickly brought Jesus to his home. When others saw this, they became visibly upset and murmured because Jesus was showing such love and honor to a sinner like Zacchaeus.

What they did not realize is that showing love, rather than judging others, brings about repentance and change of character. Zacchaeus repented of his sins and vowed to give half of his money to the poor and to repay fourfold those he had swindled. Christ's response to Zacchaeus was loving and redemptive. Luke 19:9–10 (ERV): "Jesus said, 'Today is the day for this family to be saved from sin. Yes, even this tax collector is one of God's chosen people. The Son of Man came to find lost people and save them.'"

The Bible mentions about forty-six times to greet one another, to be loving toward strangers, to greet leaders and other believers.

Meeting Guidelines
1. Smile when greeting or being greeted.
2. Maintain eye contact. This demonstrates confidence.
3. Stay calm, polite, and respectful.
4. Avoid judging and treating people by appearance or accent.
5. Use appropriate titles when meeting and greeting. Out of respect, children should refrain from calling adults by their first names; instead, use "sir," "ma'am," or "madam." If names are known, children may start with "Mr." or "Ms." or "Mrs.," then the first or last name of the adult.

International Handshake Etiquette
Handshake etiquette varies from culture to culture. Some cultures seldom give handshakes. A handshake reveals a lot. It can reveal if a person is interested in the person they are meeting or not. It can reveal if a person is respectful or not. On the other hand, refusing to give a handshake, when one has been extended to you, will be interpreted as a sign of arrogance and indifference.

1. In Thailand, the citizens put their palms together near the chest area then bow.
2. The Japanese highly respect and appreciate a bow.
3. A firm handshake is considered very rude in Turkey. Instead, the Turkish give gentle, lingering handshakes.
4. In Kenya, the type of handshake depends on the recipient. For example, when meeting elders and dignitaries, the right hand is extended while simultaneously grasping the right wrist with the left hand.

United States Handshake Etiquette

1. A handshake should not be too strong that it hurts or too loose that it conveys insecurity or rejection.
2. A firm handshake demonstrates importance and respect for oneself and others.
3. Smile when you shake someone's hand, and if seated, stand up if possible. A smile communicates you are friendly and approachable. It also puts people at ease. Standing conveys respect and interest.
4. Maintain eye contact and give your name as you extend your right hand. This communicates interest and honesty.
5. Lean slightly forward toward the person you are greeting. This communicates alertness, confidence, and interest.
6. Respect privacy boundaries, and do not come too close to the person you are greeting; otherwise, people tend to involuntarily move back.
7. When giving handshakes, the right hand should be opened with the thumb pointing upwards and the other fingers closed.
8. Handshakes are given web to web. The web is the inside part of the hand between the thumb and the forefinger. Web-to-web handshakes prevent grasping just the fingers or crunching the knuckles.
9. Fold your fingers over the other person's hand and maintain a firm handshake for about two seconds.

Assumptions Drawn from Incorrect Handshakes

1. A grip too weak is interpreted as insecure, weak, indifferent, untrustworthy, or unpredictable.
2. A grip too strong is interpreted as too aggressive or too dominating.
3. A grip too short is interpreted as indifferent, careless, nervous, uninterested, or disrespectful.
4. A grip too long is interpreted as too needy, controlling, manipulative, or clingy.

Dress Etiquette

How we dress is also an important part of meeting and greeting.

1. The Bible encourages us to **dress modestly and appropriately**.
2. How we dress and look tells others a lot about us. For example, dressing modestly conveys we respect ourselves and expect to be respected. It may also draw solicited or unsolicited attention from dubious characters. 1 Samuel 16:7 (WEB): "But Yahweh said to Samuel, 'Don't look on his face, or on the height of his stature, because I have rejected him; for I don't see as man sees. For man looks at the outward appearance, but Yahweh looks at the heart.'" We can conclude from this Scripture that how we look on the outside affects people's perception and, ultimately, affects how they treat us.
3. Cleanliness is another important part of meeting and greeting. We should do our best to look and smell clean, bathing daily and wearing clean clothes.
4. Clothes should fit properly. Avoid overly tight, overly revealing attire. Avoid short skirts and dresses, or low-cut blouses: these distract and encourage unclean thoughts.
5. Iron clothes if needed.
6. For adults, dentists recommend brushing teeth thoroughly for two minutes, at least twice daily, in the morning and at night before bed. A one-minute brushing time is acceptable for young children. Floss teeth daily. Use mouthwash. For children, age-appropriate mouthwash may be used with parental supervision.

7. Maintain a suitable hairstyle. Apply deodorant and lotion. For children, begin to use a sensitive-skin deodorant from about the age of seven or eight. Confirm the deodorant of choice with the children's pediatrician.

8. Maintain clean, manicured, or trimmed nails.

9. Wear clean and properly fitting shoes.

10. Be merciful and privately help others who may not be aware and in need of assistance with their grooming or clothing. For example, alert a sister if there is lipstick on her teeth or blouse.

Social Etiquette

1. Clean up after yourself at home and in public areas. Matthew 7:12 (WEB): "Therefore whatever you desire for men to do to you, you shall also do to them; for this is the law and the prophets."

2. After washing hands, use a paper towel to dry the sink area.

3. Even in homes with nannies, housekeepers, and cleaning services, it is wise that children learn to keep their rooms clean and are held responsible if they do not. This will teach them responsibility, respect, humility, and gratitude for what the Lord has blessed their family with.

4. Teach and encourage children to help with chores at home, in the church, or at school. Having responsibilities will help in the building of good and strong character, so the children do not grow up thinking the world revolves around them. They will learn to care about and serve others. Another benefit is that thankful people are happy people. Luke 16:10 (WEB): "He who is faithful in a very little is faithful also in much. He who is dishonest in a very little is also dishonest in much."

5. Stand up when meeting and greeting others. This shows respect, interest, and alertness. Standing up also shows both parties are of equal importance as both are at the same eye level. Those excused from standing are the elderly, those who may be unwell, or those with physical challenges. They may remain seated while greeting. Always smile. Smiling invites,

comforts, and puts people to rest. It also shows kindness and encourages conversation. Make and maintain eye contact while meeting and greeting. This shows you are confident, focused, and interested in the other party. Eye contact also demonstrates respect. Avoid waiting to be greeted. Instead, be assertive and proactive—think ahead and be a problem solver. For example, does someone need company or help? Lastly, while meeting and greeting, stay positive and alert by praying in your heart for the Lord to bless and help others.

Additional Reflection Verses

Matthew 5:47 (WEB): If you only greet your friends, what more do you do than others? Don't even the tax collectors do the same?

Romans 12:16 (NLT): Live in harmony with each other. Don't be too proud to enjoy the company of ordinary people. And don't think you know it all!

Chapter 11

Spiritual Etiquette

Biblical Foundation
Let not mercy and truth forsake you; Bind them around your neck, Write them on the tablet of your heart, And so find favor and high esteem In the sight of God and man.
(PROVERBS 3:3–4 NKJV)

Spiritual etiquette has to do with principles that govern our souls. Our souls are made up of three parts: the mind, emotions, and will. Through prayer and obedience to the Word of God, spiritual etiquette involves taking personal responsibility over what one thinks, how they feel, and the choices they make. It includes breaking bad habits by using biblical principles and learning good behavior.

The battle begins in the mind with our thoughts. If we are defeated there, negative and disturbing emotions or desires flood the heart. If pollution of the mind and heart continue unchecked, negative suggestions to solve the perceived problems are sent back to the mind to tempt us to say and do wrong, destructive things. Continuing to dwell on negative, angry, unforgiving, or dirty thoughts will produce negative emotions that produce more negative thoughts that lead to making wrong decisions and choices. This is the reason we hear of horrifying stories about children harming other children, or teenagers shooting their schoolmates, or adults shooting innocent people at public events. Often they've allowed their bitterness or anger to overcome their bodies, acting out the thoughts that have been caged in their heads.

An excellent story that shows what can happen to anyone if we allow our minds to go unchecked is the story of David and Bathsheba. We see the stages of sin developing in King David when he committed adultery with Bathsheba in 2 Samuel 11. He saw her—Uriah's wife—bathing and did not turn away. He should have stopped there, looked away, but he did not. As he continued to gaze, thoughts of lust flooded his mind, which produced feelings of lust in his heart. King David's heart deceived him by providing an evil solution to his lusting problem. He asked who the woman was and was clearly informed that she was the wife of Uriah, but that did not stop him. Again, God provided an honorable solution by giving David a way of escape from the temptation, but once again, David, a man of God, was blinded by lust.

This is also a lesson that any believer in Christ, no matter how strong in God, can fall. Scripture tells us that pride comes before destruction. No one is so high in God that they do not need to obey God's Word. David's heart deceived his mind into believing that since he was king, he could get away with enjoying another man's wife. After all, the fighting men were away at war, while their wives were left home alone. Who would know? Who would dare challenge the king?

The story goes on to tell us that David had Bathsheba brought to him, and he committed adultery with her. After some time, Bathsheba sent word to David that she was pregnant. Again, David's mind and heart deceived him into believing he could "solve" the problem. He deceptively called for Uriah to return from the battlefield, hoping that Uriah would spend some time at home with his wife, Bathsheba, so David's secret sin with her could remain secret. David commanded his general, Joab, to send Uriah to him. When Uriah arrived, David asked him to give a report of the status of the war efforts against the Ammonites, then encouraged him to go home and relax. Instead, to King David's dismay, Uriah slept at the palace entrance along with the king's servants!

King David questioned Uriah, but the principled soldier explained that he was unwilling to go visit his wife because he could not bear the thought of enjoying himself while his fellow soldiers were risking their lives in battle.

It is sad and disturbing to observe that King David did not think the same honoring way of his soldiers who were fighting, dying, and sacrificing their comforts for him at war against the Ammonites. We are told earlier in the chapter of 2 Samuel 11, when the story begins, that David did not go out to war with his soldiers, as was customary of kings at that time. Rather than going to war with his soldiers, we find David arising from bed late in the afternoon and wandering about on the roof of his palace. King David had become proud, complacent, and lax . . . a perfect target for Satan's deception.

God abhors sin because it steals, kills, and destroys. King David tried everything he could, including getting Uriah drunk, but alas, Uriah, determined and resolute, continued to sleep at the palace entrance. Finally, desperate and blinded by evil, David made a most destructive choice that brought God's swift judgment upon himself and his household. He sent Uriah back to the battlefield with his own execution letter in hand! The letter was delivered to Joab, his general, instructing him to position Uriah at the frontlines of the battle, close to the city wall, where it was most dangerous, then abandon him to guarantee his death. After Ammonite soldiers killed Uriah, David sent a message back to Joab, the general of his army, telling him not to be discouraged, for "the sword devours this one today and that one tomorrow! Fight harder next time and conquer the city!" (2 Samuel 11:25 NLT).

After the customary period of mourning had passed, King David took Bathsheba and made her his wife. The Bible tells us that God was very displeased with all the evil David had done and promised that the sword would never leave his household. The child conceived with Bathsheba in adultery died after birth. One of David's sons, Amnon, developed lustful feelings for his own sister, Tamar, and per the evil advice of his evil cousin Jonadab, raped her. Absalom, another son of David, avenged Tamar by having his servants kill Amnon. Absalom rebelled against his father, David, in a coup, deceiving and dividing the people, and attempted to steal the kingdom. King David fled from Jerusalem because of his son's rebellion. Absalom temporarily occupied his father's throne in Jerusalem and raped his father's secondary wives in public. Absalom was viciously murdered at general Joab's command, despite King David's command that he should not be harmed. No one, including this man after God's heart, gets away with sin.

Secret sins, no matter how big or small, are totally visible and contemptible to God and will bring a curse not only to the individual but to descendants as well if there's no repentance. It's crucial we repent and turn away from sin and ask for forgiveness in Jesus's name; otherwise, sooner or later, judgment is certain. Thankfully, David repented for what he had done, and God spared his life from death and restored him to a right standing with God. The good news for us today is that our sins can be washed away and forgotten by a loving God. The Bible tells that He loved the world so much that He gave His Son, Jesus, that whosoever believes in him will not perish, but have eternal life. Accepting the work of Christ through His life, death on the cross, and resurrection brings redemption. Micah 7:18–20 (BBE):

Who is a God like you, offering forgiveness for evil-doing and overlooking the sins of the rest of his heritage? he does not keep his wrath for ever, because his delight is in mercy. He will again have pity on us; he will put our sins under his feet: and you will send all our sins down into the heart of the sea. You will make clear your good faith to Jacob and your mercy to Abraham, as you gave your oath to our fathers from times long past.

Spiritual Guidelines

As with David, we all are in a spiritual war against evil forces because we live in a fallen world. The only way to win is to lean upon the mighty arm of the Lord through prayer and obeying the Word of God. Immediately upon awaking in the morning, I recommend following this regimen to fight the daily attacks of the Evil One against our families, churches, communities, and world:

1. Start by greeting and thanking the Holy Spirit.
2. Cover your mind, heart, and will with the blood of Jesus Christ. Cover your body and spirit too.
3. Cover your entire family and possessions with the blood of Jesus Christ. Revelation 12:11 (BBE): "And they overcame him through the blood of the Lamb and the word of their witness; and loving not their lives they freely gave themselves up to death."
4. Ask the Holy Spirit to guide you through the day and remind you to pray for others, including government leaders, spiritual leaders, first responders, the military, children, families, neighbors, etc.

5. A lifestyle of daily prayer and obedience to God's commands will guard our hearts and minds from Satan's lies and trickery. It will also keep us humble, teachable, and accountable to God and others.

6. Stay grounded in a Bible-believing church. Paul describes the armor of God for the believer: the belt of truth, the breastplate of righteousness, the shoes of the gospel of peace, the shield of faith, the helmet of salvation, and the sword of the spirit. Note that he does not mention protective gear for the soldiers back . . . that's because the people of God cover each other in prayer. No soldier goes to battle alone. We mourn together. We rejoice together. We also learn to fight spiritual battles together and win.

Additional Reflection Verses

1. Deuteronomy 4:9 (BBE): Only take care, and keep watch on your soul, for fear that the things which your eyes have seen go from your memory and from your heart all the days of your life; but let the knowledge of them be given to your children and to your children's children.

2. 1 Thessalonians 5:16–18 (KJV): Rejoice evermore. Pray without ceasing. In every thing give thanks: for this is the will of God in Christ Jesus concerning you.

3. 1 Peter 5:8–9 (NLT): Stay alert! Watch out for your great enemy, the devil. He prowls around like a roaring lion, looking for someone to devour. Stand firm against him, and be strong in your faith. Remember that your family of believers all over the world is going through the same kind of suffering you are.

Chapter 12

Personal Etiquette

Biblical Foundation

Put on therefore, as God's chosen ones, holy and beloved, a heart of compassion, kindness, lowliness, humility, and perseverance; bearing with one another, and forgiving each other, if any man has a complaint against any; even as Christ forgave you, so you also do. Above all these things, walk in love, which is the bond of perfection.
(COLOSSIANS 3:12–14 WEB)

Opening Doors

Opening doors for others is an act of kindness. It shows we respect and care about other people.

1. The response to someone opening the door is a smile and eye contact and ends with a verbal and enthusiastic "Thank you!" Many times I add, "God bless you," remembering the promise by the Lord to Abraham and his descendants in Genesis 12:3 (WEB): "I will bless those who bless you, and I will curse him who curses you. All the families of the earth will be blessed through you." It is an opportunity to bless others and remind the Good Lord to bless them.

2. In general, the person who gets to the door first opens and holds it for the next person.
3. A gentleman walks ahead to open the door for a lady.
4. For doors that open outward: Open the door by pulling it toward you and standing behind it to allow the person behind to pass.
5. For doors that open inward: A gentleman will push the door open, go through it, then stand behind the door to allow the lady to pass. If a lady is already at the door and opening it, simply open it wider. The lady responds with eye contact, a smile, and a verbal "Thank you."
6. If someone has their hands full or is pushing a stroller, always offer to open the door for them regardless of gender.
7. In a situation where you get caught holding the door open and many people start to enter, make eye contact with someone, smile, and say, "Here you go." Slowly let the door slip from your fingers so it does not hit anyone.
8. When someone is in a wheelchair, ask, "May I get the door?" and wait for their response before proceeding.
9. When it comes to opening car doors, gentlemen open car doors for ladies by pulling the door out and standing behind as the lady enters. A gentleman may offer to carry or hold what a lady is carrying, including a purse, until she's settled in the car. Make sure all is safely in and tucked away, including dress and skirt edges, before shutting the door.

Phone Etiquette

Phone etiquette shows us how to communicate effectively with respect, consideration, and patience for the people we talk with. It is especially important to have good manners over the phone because we cannot see the other person's facial expressions and body language, and unless we are using a video calling feature, they can't see us. It becomes even more important to choose our words carefully and use more tone inflections in our voices to compensate.

The most successful companies are the ones with great customer service that permit their customers to interact with courteous representatives. More commonly in business, we are greeted by an impersonal automated message that leads to selecting a number and then another number from another menu that leads to yet another menu. We get desperate to speak to a real human being, and sometimes when we do, we are alarmed to find the person lacks the basics of good manners.

Just as we teach our children how to behave in public, it is also important that we teach them phone etiquette. It starts with us as parents making sure we demonstrate good phone etiquette because our children are watching.

With many children receiving cell phones today, it's important as parents we set parental control systems, especially with the internet. Parents should check their children's phones unannounced and regularly. Time limits should be set. Let's be particularly vigilant as parents and guardians. So many children stumble upon inappropriate material on the internet. In the November 2016 article "The Impact of Media Use and Screen Time on Children, Adolescents, and Families," the American College of Pediatricians (ACPeds) reports that "visual images can also be frightening for the young child—and these images can remain in the child's sub conscious for a long time, causing nightmares and other sleep disturbances."[1]

Another concern is that there are crafty people who target children with inappropriate, predatory advertising or pretend to be children on video games. Let's be vigilant and attentive as parents and guardians. Cybersex has become a grave concern among children. In that same article, ACPeds describes cybersex as "a virtual sex encounter between persons remotely connected via a computer network . . . [where] participants pretend they are having sexual relations. These computer

---

[1] https://www.acpeds.org/the-college-speaks/position-statements/parenting-issues/the-impact-of-media-use-and-screen-time-on-children-adolescents-and-families.

sites are available to all who desire access, including children. The Internet also plays a growing role in sex crimes committed against children. These crimes range from sexual exploitation, such as child pornography, to actual assault against a victim identified through the Internet." Cybersex is also used as a bullying tool among some adolescents who send and receive nude or almost nude photos of themselves on their phones. The article also reported a study that showed that "22 percent of teen girls said they have sent partially nude or fully nude photos of themselves, and 18 percent of boys have done so. Adolescents adversely impacted by cybersex/bullying often suffer from lower school grades, anxiety, alcohol and drug use, depression, and rarely, suicidal ideation and suicide. Adolescents sharing such photographs could be prosecuted for being in possession of child pornography."

Phone Guidelines for Children

1. Unless it's the grandparents calling, toddlers should not answer the phone. This creates frustration to the caller.

2. Let children practice good phone etiquette with their parents first. People are impressed and will remember, especially in our world today, when children have good manners.

3. For child safety reasons, children should not give their names or home addresses over the phone. In our family, we don't allow our young children to answer the phone unless we see who is calling. If it's a loving relative or trusted family friend, yes; otherwise, no.

4. If the name of the person calling is known, children may say, "Good morning, Uncle Smith!"

5. To end the call with a relative or family friend, children may say, "I'm so happy to hear from you, Ms. Smith" or "How wonderful to hear from you, Aunt Lucy; I will let Mom know you called."

Phone Guidelines in General

1. Smile when speaking over the phone. The voice sounds much more pleasant.

2. Avoid yelling, intimidating, and threatening speech. This kind of behavior exposes a person as deeply insecure, abusive, and controlling. If a conversation gets heated, use good judgment and end the conversation immediately. Take time to calm down, and if it's business, call back and speak to a different agent or seek help through the company's website.

3. Control your emotions and refrain from using vulgar or obscene language.

4. As much as possible, speak directly into the phone and not while on speaker. Two reasons: background noises are reduced, and it feels safer and more respectful to the other person that their information is kept between the two of you.

5. If with other people and you must answer your phone, excuse yourself to speak in private.

Employee Etiquette

Employee or office etiquette has to do with the rules that govern respectful behavior at the workplace. Get the dress-code information from the human resources department. Here are some things to remember:

1. Respect and support the vision and mission of the organization by always representing it with an excellent work ethic and a good attitude.

2. Answer phones courteously and return calls promptly.

3. Use correct grammar in office correspondence, including texts and emails.

4. With texts, casual language and abbreviated words are permissible.

5. Dress appropriately.

6. Be on time or early.

7. Smile and greet everyone enthusiastically, from the parking lot attendants, to the security people at the door, to the receptionist at the front desk, to your colleagues and bosses.

8. Avoid cliques. Respect everyone.

9. Help others, including holding open doors, carrying items, serving coffee.

10. Welcome and help new colleagues feel comfortable.

11. Avoid gossips and complainers.

12. Be kind, honest, and courteous to everyone, including coworkers, janitors, lunch attendants, maintenance staff. Always say "Please," "Thank you," "You're welcome."

13. Be neat and clean.

14. Remain respectful to all and avoid offensive or obscene behavior, discussions, and materials. This is sexual harassment; it's evil and it's illegal.

15. Avoid sexist comments or jokes.

16. Use company computers, email, and supplies for work and not personal use.

17. Remain thankful for your job, and work with excellence, finishing projects on time.

18. Refrain from chewing and popping gum. It's annoying and distracting to others.

19. Follow the chain of command.

20. If truly sick, ask for the day off so as not to spread sickness to others, but don't use sick days for personal time.

21. Sneeze into a tissue or your elbow, then say, "Excuse me." The response should be "God bless you."

22. Avoid eating strong-smelling foods in the office.

23. Always knock and wait to be acknowledged before entering someone's office.

24. Stay busy with your work and avoid interrupting others, unless necessary. Always apologize for interrupting.

25. Be thankful when others help you.

26. Speak clearly without yelling.

27. Avoid hanging around or hovering over a coworker while they are working or on the phone. If busy, leave a note for them to get back to you.

28. Be compassionate and discreet when correcting others. Remember to treat others as you would want to be treated.

29. Take immediate responsibility for your mistakes and apologize. Don't blame others. If you're not sure, apologize anyway. Do everything you can to correct the mistake.

30. If your work is criticized by the boss, stay calm and find out what exactly is wrong with it. If you disagree, discuss with respect but defer to the boss's opinion. Of course, no superior should mislead or threaten a subordinate to do anything immoral, unethical, or illegal. That's evil and against the law.

31. At meetings avoid dominating and interrupting others. This is disrespectful and inconsiderate.

32. Refrain from sighing with boredom, shuffling papers, or falling asleep at meetings.

33. Refrain from walking out of meetings; wait until the person in charge closes.

34. Respect older individuals. We can all learn something.

35. Leave the office bathrooms clean for others. Do the same with the office kitchen.

36. Mute cell phones. It is inappropriate to make or receive calls at a meeting unless it is pertinent to your business.

37. If you must take a call, go outside or find a quiet place where you can talk without disturbing coworkers.

Employer Etiquette

Employer etiquette governs how employers or bosses treat their employees. Employees should be treated with respect and dignity.

1. Be the example by dressing appropriately.

2. Be kind, honest, and courteous to all employees, including janitors, lunch workers, maintenance staff.

3. Always say "Please," "Thank you," "You're welcome."

4. Maintain the same standards of job expectations for every employee.

5. Provide a safe working environment by not tolerating discrimination, sexism, cliques, bullying, etc.

6. Stay calm, exercise patience, and listen to an employee when they make suggestions for improvement or give reasons for why they did their work a certain way.

7. Be compassionate and discreet when correcting employees. Remember to treat others as you would want to be treated.

8. Handle disagreements with sensitivity and tact.

9. Refrain from minimizing or humiliating employees when they express an idea, or you will lose the respect of your employees.

10. As much as possible, know the names of your employees and remember specific information about them.

11. Help welcome new employees by introducing them to the other employees.

12. Keep private information private.

13. Give clear instructions of what you expect from each employee.

14. Provide continuing education or training.

15. Be approachable for questions and clarification by being courteous and respectful.

16. Pay your employees correctly and on time.

17. Encourage, compliment, and celebrate employees for a job well done, plus give bonuses.

18. Stay honest and ethical with business decisions behind the scenes.

Hat Etiquette

Hat etiquette is still important today depending on where you go and where you are—for example, it is impolite for men to keep their hats on when the national anthem is being played.

A hat or cap consists of a crown and brim.

1. To tip your hat means to hold the brim of the hat and lift it a few inches off your head toward the person you are greeting. It also means to hold the brim with your forefinger and thumb and tug it forward briefly. Sometimes the tipping of the hat is done by briefly lifting the hat by the crown. The tipping of the hat with a slight bow is a nonverbal greeting of recognition and respect.

2. To "doff your hat" means to completely remove your hat as a sign of respect when being introduced or when stopping to speak to someone, especially a lady.

3. If the conversation continues for more than a minute, then the hat may be placed back on the head. This is known as "donning your hat," which means to put on your hat. For men, any ornament attachments are placed on the left side of the hat.

4. In Western cultures like the United States and England, men take their hats off (including baseball caps):
   - ✓ At a table to eat
   - ✓ When they enter most buildings, including homes; churches; restaurants; theaters; government or public institutions like a courthouse, library, or school. Hats can be left on when outdoors, at indoor and outdoor sports events, and in certain public buildings like hotels, airports, and post offices.
   - ✓ At the passing of the flag of the United States and during the national anthem. The right hand removes the hat from your head and puts it on your left shoulder, so your right hand is over your heart. The hat should be held in such a way that the inside lining is not visible to others.
   - ✓ At funerals or the passing of a funeral cortege, at indoor and outdoor weddings, and at other important formal occasions.

5. In Western culture, women are not required to take off their hats indoors or outdoors because their hats are considered attire-specific items.

   ✓ Women keep their hats on at the playing of the national anthem and at the passing of the flag of the United States. The exemption is when wearing baseball-style caps that are traditionally considered for men; in this case, women are to follow the same hat rules as men.

   ✓ For women, any ornament attachments are placed on the right side of the hat.

6. Having traveled to many countries, including Israel, Turkey, Qatar, and the United Arab Emirates, we have found that some of these cultures require both men and women to wear head coverings indoors and outdoors.

   ✓ In the Jewish synagogues, men wear a *kippah*, which is a round head covering, recognizing that God is the head of the family and nation.

   ✓ Many Muslim and Hindu men and women wear head coverings in mosques, temples, at work, in restaurants, and in the home.

Flag Etiquette

Flag etiquette is similar in all countries worldwide, as the flag of each country is symbolic of its citizens' great accomplishments, triumphs, and rights over territory. Flags' unique designs represent who the united people are, their values and freedoms, and where they belong. Flags conjure up deep emotions of pride for one's country and common national goals.

1. At the United Nations, the countries' flags are arranged in alphabetical order.

2. No one country's flag has precedence over another country's flag.

3. One country's flag is never flown above another country's flag on the same staff.

Flag Etiquette in the United States

1. For civilians, always respect the flag by standing and placing your right hand over your heart.
2. Those in uniform, members of the military, and veterans show respect by giving a military salute.
3. No drawings or words are permitted on the flag.
4. The flag should be displayed on a flagpole only and never used as a decorative item.
5. The flag should never be worn as clothing, a costume, or uniform.

Flag Display

1. When hoisting or raising the flag, it is done briskly and lowered ceremonially.
2. When the flag is hoisted to half the flag pole, it's called "half-staff" or "half-mast." Half-staff occurs on Memorial Day to remember those who gave their lives for the country's freedoms. It also occurs when the president or governor calls for a time of mourning.
3. To lower a flag at half-staff, it is first raised to the peak of the flag pole before lowering it.
4. Fold the flag into a triangle with the union (blue area with stars) showing, and store in a dark area with little humidity.
5. The flag is not allowed to touch the ground.
6. The flag flown upside down denotes distress.
7. The US flag flies highest, followed by the state flag, military flag, then other flags of the nation.
8. The national flag is hoisted first and lowered last.

9. When displaying the US flag outside at night, shine a light on it. If no light is available, take the flag down at sunset and hoist it at sunrise.

10. The US flag is flown at the same height as other national flags.

11. If the US flag is placed on a wall or window, the union (blue area with white stars) must face the observer's left.

Disposing of the US Flag

1. Disposing a worn-out US flag is done with great honor and dignity.
2. A large enough fire is set outside in a safe area.
3. The flag is folded and placed in the fire.
4. The participants salute the flag and say the Pledge of Allegiance, after which there is a moment of silence as the people reflect on what the flag symbolizes.
5. After the fire is safely put out, the ashes of the flag are collected and buried in a respectful location.

Tipping Etiquette

In the American culture, tipping is the norm and is expected. It is a way of showing gratitude for the service. In Europe tipping is not mandatory. In Japan tipping is rude.

General American Guidelines for Tipping

1. At a sit-down restaurant, tip 15–20 percent or more before taxes. If the service is poor, tip 10 percent pretax.
2. At a buffet restaurant, tip 10 percent before taxes.
3. No tip necessary for takeout.
4. For home delivery, tip 10 to 15 percent pretax.
5. For valet returning your car to you, tip $2 to $5.
6. For restroom attendants tip 50 cents or more, depending on the level of service.

I have learned to carry some extra cash when traveling for tips at airports, hotels, and when taking a taxi.

Tipping Guidelines at Airports and Hotels
1. Leave $2 or more dollars per day for hotel housekeeping and a thank you note.
2. Tip airport luggage attendant $1 or $2 per bag.
3. Tip a doorman $2 for carrying luggage or helping with a cab.
4. Tip the concierge 10 to 20 percent of the price for show or tour tickets, and about $5 for restaurant reservations.
5. Tip taxi drivers 15 to 20 percent of the fare.
6. For nail and hair salons, tip 15 to 20 percent.

Additional Refection Verses

Matthew 12:33–37 (BBE): Make the tree good, and its fruit good; or make the tree bad, and its fruit bad; for by its fruit you will get knowledge of the tree. You offspring of snakes, how are you, being evil, able to say good things? because out of the heart's store come the words of the mouth. The good man out of his good store gives good things; and the evil man out of his evil store gives evil things. And I say to you that in the day when they are judged, men will have to give an account of every foolish word they have said. For by your words will your righteousness be seen, and by your words you will be judged.

Hebrews 4:13 (WEB): There is no creature that is hidden from his sight, but all things are naked and laid open before the eyes of him to whom we must give an account.

Chapter 13
Family Etiquette

Biblical Foundation

But now is the time to get rid of anger, rage, malicious behavior, slander, and dirty language. Don't lie to each other, for you have stripped off your old sinful nature and all its wicked deeds. Put on your new nature, and be renewed as you learn to know your Creator and become like him.
(COLOSSIANS 3:8–10 NLT)

Kenyans are friendly people, and family is important. Part of my upbringing that I have carried into my married and parenting life is the importance of working as a team. No one person does all the work. Everyone shares in the responsibility, for example, of keeping our home clean with the understanding that we are simply stewards of God's blessings. Creating a peaceful home atmosphere is key and honors the Lord. Everyone in the family is important and has a major role to play for the harmony and success of the family. When my mother cooked, I was by her side hearing stories and watching as she prepared each meal. I learned early how to take care of others by serving. Having relatives and friends visit often is a normal Kenyan way of life. The doors are always open unless someone is a troublemaker.

My husband and I believe in the importance of leading our children by example, which means that for our children to be respectful, we must show respect to each other as spouses. If we want our children to demonstrate godly, respectful manners, it means our children must see the same in us, their parents, in daily home life. Our character as parents at the church, at the workplace, and with neighbors and friends should be similar behind closed doors. The only way for our family to grow in virtue has been through prayer and the meditation on the Word of God as a family.

Family etiquette are the guidelines that govern how we treat and interact with the family members with whom we live. Scripture teaches us in 1 Corinthians 13 that God's kind of love produces the kind of behavior that keeps families united and in harmony. Rage and abusive language are not from God and only bring what Satan wants, which is division, strife, and destruction of the family unit. The love of Christ produces respect, kindness, forgiveness, gentleness, and patience. When we accept Christ as our Lord and Savior and begin to pray and meditate on Scripture, our minds are transformed into a Christlike mindset.

Etiquette in the Home

1. A great way to develop godly character in us and our children is by starting the day with prayer. Children can say a short prayer and then proceed to greet parents or elders before doing other things like eating, playing, doing chores, or preparing for school. This behavior is part of good manners and demonstrates honor, humility, and gratitude. I teach and encourage my children to say, "Good morning, Holy Spirit. Thank You for today," before getting out of bed, to avoid forgetting.

2. Thanksgiving prayers are important, as they acknowledge that God is King and our total dependence is on Him as our Lord. Matthew 22:37–40 (NLT): "Jesus replied, 'You must love the Lord your God with all your heart, all your soul, and all your mind.' This is the first and greatest commandment. A second is equally important: 'Love your neighbor as yourself.' The entire law and all the demands of the prophets are based on these two commandments."

3. The demonstration of good manners always begins with the Lord. If technology, entertainment, and other people take so much of our time, hence treated as more important than God, they are idols. Bowing down to idols is idolatry. Exodus 20:3 (BBE): "You are to have no other gods but me." If we treat the Lord with honor, we will treat others with honor because every good thing and way come from God.

4. It is good manners for children to greet their parents in the morning upon arising. This shows the parents respect and gratitude for all they do and endure. After their greeting, communicate and confirm what chores are to be completed.

5. It is good manners for children to meet and greet their parents at the door when they return home from work, shopping, or another event. Wherever the children are in the house, whatever they are doing, they are to stop, even if it is in the middle of a great game or a great show, then go and meet and greet their parents.

6. Parents should lead by example, especially when it comes to time spent viewing emails, social media, blogging, streaming music and movies, and surfing the internet. These activities, if left unchecked for a long period, can cause a rift in families due to neglect and frustrations. Children do what they see their parents doing and children left alone to freely surf the internet is dangerous. Many have been lured into horrifying and illegal activities. Parents spending time with their children and vice versa is much more important than any social media or any celebrity lifestyle.

7. It is a great blessing to encourage and praise one's parents often, not just on birthdays or when receiving gifts. Parents can demonstrate this by speaking blessings over each other as spouses, speaking blessings over the children, and speaking blessings over their own parents. Proverbs 31:28 (WEB): "Her children rise up and call her blessed. Her husband also praises her." It is a great blessing and relief to parents when they see that their children are thoughtful, respectful, grateful, and appreciative of them.

8. One way children can demonstrate love and respect for their parents is by assisting them with bringing in items, briefcases, and groceries when they arrive home. This habit melts hearts and brings greater joy and unity in the home.

9. Show mercy and kindness by asking parents how their day was and if they need help with anything. Proverbs 3:3 (WEB): "Don't let kindness and truth forsake you. Bind them around your neck. Write them on the tablet of your heart."

10. It is easier for children to remember to use kind words like "Please," "Thank you," and "You're welcome" routinely in conversation if they hear their parents using them. The same goes with acts of kindness: it is easier for children to use polite language, or assist parents with putting away groceries, or setting the table if they see parents demonstrating the same kindness to others in the family, workplace, and church.

11. Training begins at home. Children will repeat and imitate what they see and hear at home. What is happening in the home will eventually come to light. Bad habits will harm the family and community, while the development of good and godly habits will produce great blessings for the family and community at large. Proverbs 23:24 (NLT): "The father of godly children has cause for joy. What a pleasure to have children who are wise."

Receiving Visitors at Home

Similar guidelines apply when guests come to visit:

1. We cheerfully meet and greet guests at the door and assist with bringing in their items.

2. Children are to be present to cheerfully receive guests and not so busy and distracted playing games or watching shows—such items are paused or switched off to give full attention to visitors and their children.

3. Once pleasantries have been exchanged, then the children are released to designated areas to play together.

4. Guests are never to be ignored, but treated with love, respect, and appreciation in one's home.

5. All guests are included in wholesome discussions and games.

6. Avoid ignoring guests when they visit.

7. Avoid speaking in unknown languages that include some and isolate others. It is terribly rude to ignore guests when they have taken time to come and visit you.

8. Children are to give parents privacy to speak to their friends. They say, "Excuse me, please," when needing to communicate something and waiting patiently to be acknowledged.

9. Children can help parents by watching over and keeping the visiting children in designated play areas.

10. All activities—video games, watching shows, listening to music, playing outside, swimming—should be age appropriate and preapproved by parents.

11. Due to the risk of accidents and damaging of property, discourage children from jumping on couches, ottomans, tables, or beds.

12. Wandering into private rooms is unacceptable. Children locking themselves in bedrooms or bathrooms with other people's children is unacceptable. Bedroom doors are always left wide open.

13. Children should always feel free to alert grown-ups if there has been an accident or they are not sure about a game or show. Err on the side of caution rather than on the fear of offending.

14. Being righteous is about doing the right thing even when no one is looking. This demonstrates character and maturity.

15. After playing, children are to guide their friends in cleaning up and putting away toys.

Etiquette at Someone Else's House

We are to be our best in character and attitude when visiting others in their homes, to facilitate a delightful experience for all. This will not only bless the host but also leave a good impression that strengthens the bond of the relationship. Proverbs 22:1 (BBE): "A good name is more to be desired than great wealth, and to be respected is better than silver and gold."

1. Parents should have already trained and discussed with the children, ahead of time, how they are expected to behave when visiting others.

2. How children behave in their own home is the way they will behave in another person's house. So if they throw toys from the second floor to the first in their own home, damaging walls and floors, with no correction and no discipline from their parents, they will repeat the same behavior elsewhere. If the children scratch and draw on walls, they will do the same when visiting others. If they bully and abuse their own siblings, they will do the same with other people's children. Proverbs 19:18 (NLT): "Discipline your children while there is hope. Otherwise you will ruin their lives."

3. When the host or hostess greets and welcomes you into their home, respond in kind with a smile, a firm handshake, or hug depending on the level of acquaintance, and give a positive verbal response. For example: "I am fine, thank you! Thank you for inviting us!"

4. Out of respect for the host and their home, remove your shoes, unless the host absolutely insists otherwise. Always respect and follow the host.

5. In many cultures, removing shoes in the home is a sign of cleanliness, respect, and humility. You'll observe this especially

with Asian, Indian, Muslim, and African families. A person's home is their sanctuary, so observing, following, and confirming with the host what is respectful to them is important. A 2008 study conducted by the University of Arizona showed the dangers of wearing outside shoes in the home. They deposit all kinds of dangerous contaminants, including pollutants like oils and chemicals and dangerous bacteria and filth. The study found over 400,000 bacteria, including E. coli and others picked up from public bathrooms and grass, which cause all kinds of health problems, including respiratory and urinary tract problems.[2] Need I say more? To reduce these problems, leave shoes at the door, vacuum regularly, and use steam mops on floors to destroy most of these dangerous bacteria.

6. There are times when removing shoes may not be appropriate— for example, when holding a public formal gathering in one's home such as a political meeting, a wedding, or a reception. In these cases, and similar, remove area rugs or hold the meeting in a yard with sufficient and comfortable sitting arrangements for your guests.

7. We reap what we sow. Respecting others will produce a harvest of the same—others will also respect us and our homes. Matthew 7:12 (BBE): "All those things, then, which you would have men do to you, even so do you to them: because this is the law and the prophets."

8. Ask the host where personal items should be hanged or kept. Some homes have coat closets. Personal items include hats, coats, bags, and umbrellas.

9. Children are to use inside voices inside the home, and when outside, louder voices are acceptable.

10. With closed doors, especially bathrooms and bedrooms, always knock and wait to be acknowledged before entering. If there's no answer, open the door cautiously.

11. Wait to be given something to eat and drink, and be grateful.

---

[2] Sheri Maxwell, B.S., Charles P. Gerba, Ph. D. "Shoe Study." Department of Soil, Water and Environmental Science, University of Arizona, Tuscon, Arizona, March 31, 2008.

12. Compliment the host.
13. Table manners matter—use inside voices, keep elbows off the table, eat small bites at a time with mouth closed, and avoid speaking with the mouth full.
14. Offer to help with cleanup.
15. Continue to use "May I," "Please," "Thank you," and "You're welcome" routinely.

Etiquette at Stores, Schools, Restaurants, and Other Public Settings

We are to be our best in character and attitude, showing respect and gratitude to the people who serve us in public. It starts at home with the way we treat our family members and the language we use. If we are thoughtful, respectful, and gracious in private, we will be the same way in public.

General Guidelines in Public

1. Always use polite, respectful language with the people who serve us—cashiers, waiters, and waitresses; first responders, like the police; all government officials; and teachers. Etiquette begins at home with the way we speak to each other and the way we speak about others.
2. Hateful, prejudiced speech and behavior have no place in our homes or anywhere else. Children learn these negative, destructive behaviors, then repeat them at school.
3. Even though we do not always agree on opinions, we can learn to express ourselves respectfully and constructively. Proverbs 25:15 (*Voice*): "Patience can soften up a leader, and a tender tongue can break *even* bone."
4. Children are to use formal greetings and responses with adults and always start with the appropriate titles and names, if known; otherwise use "ma'am" or "sir."
5. In many countries, especially in Europe, Africa, and Asia, "madam" is used for women.

6. An example of a formal general greeting: "How do you do, Pastor Smith." When asked the same, the correct response is, "How do you do, Ms. Mary." This is a greeting, not a question.

7. A formal morning greeting: "Good morning, Ms. Smith."

8. A formal afternoon greeting: "Good afternoon, sir."

9. A formal evening greeting: "Good evening, ma'am."

10. In the United States, greetings are generally informal, so "Hi," "Hello," "How are you?" and "How are you doing?" are often used. Correct responses for children to adults: "I am fine, thank you, sir," or, "I am well, thank you, ma'am."

Additional Reflection Verses

Matthew 6:14–15 (WEB): For if you forgive men their trespasses, your heavenly Father will also forgive you. But if you don't forgive men their trespasses, neither will your Father forgive your trespasses.

Colossians 3:12–15 (NLT): Since God chose you to be the holy people he loves, you must clothe yourselves with tenderhearted mercy, kindness, humility, gentleness, and patience. Make allowance for each other's faults, and forgive anyone who offends you. Remember, the Lord forgave you, so you must forgive others. Above all, clothe yourselves with love, which binds us all together in perfect harmony. And let the peace that comes from Christ rule in your hearts. For as members of one body you are called to live in peace. And always be thankful.

Chapter 14

Table Etiquette

Biblical Foundation

*After the queen of Sh'va had seen all Shlomo's wisdom,
the palace he had built, the food at his table, the
manner of seating his officials, the manner in which
his staff served him, how they were dressed, his personal
servants and his burnt offering which he offered
in the house of Adonai, it left her breathless.*
(1 KINGS 10:4–5 CJB)

Table etiquette is as equally important as the meal prepared. The time and care it takes to decorate and set a table demonstrate love, hard work, and thoughtfulness for going out of one's way to make the mealtime as comfortable and enjoyable as possible. Such care also demonstrates honor and respect for the guests. Gathering at the table for a meal is one of the most enjoyable activities we engage in. It is at the table that the family comes together. It is at the table that experiences are shared and memories are forged for a lifetime.

Table etiquette includes good manners along with guidelines for arranging the table with tableware for serving and eating. An easy way to remember how to set a table is to picture the word "FORKS" from left to right, minus the R. "F" for the fork on the left of the plate. "O" for the shape of the plate. "K" for the knife on the right of the plate, the sharp edge always facing the plate. "S" for the spoon, which goes by the knife. The bread and butter plate is placed above the fork. To remember where the bread and butter plate is placed and where the glass is placed, hold out your hands in front of you and touch the tips of your thumbs to the tips of your forefingers to make a lowercase "b" with your left hand and a lowercase "d" with your right hand. This reminds you the "bread and butter" go to the left of the place setting and "drinks" go to the right. The glass is placed above the knife. The napkin is placed to the left of the fork, under the fork, or on the plate.

Table Manners

1. Maintain proper table posture by sitting upright.
2. Gentlemen take off their hats, and ladies place their handbags or purses by their feet or on their lap. Ladies are not obligated to take off their hats.
3. Feet are kept on the floor.
4. Move up slightly on your chair to prevent bending over food or plate.
5. Rest your hands on your lap. Forearms may be rested on the table, but not elbows. Elbows are kept to your side.
6. Show respect and appreciation for others at the dinner table by turning off electronic devices and putting them away from the table.
7. Unfold your napkin and place it on your lap as soon as you sit down.
8. Napkins are for patting the lips, not wiping the nose, so excuse yourself and go to the bathroom as needed.
9. Use lively but not overly loud voices.

10. Conversations should include all guests; no cliques at the table.

11. Don't start eating until everyone has been served.

12. Out of respect for the host's hard work, taste your food before asking for salt and pepper.

13. Take small bites and place the knife and fork down on plate between bites. Used silverware should be placed on the plate, not the table.

14. Chew quietly with your mouth closed.

15. Allow others to finish chewing before asking questions.

16. Avoid talking with food in your mouth, as it may be visible to others as you are speaking, or you may accidentally choke on it.

17. If a dish platter or bowl is outside your personal eating space, avoid reaching over others; rather, ask that the dish be passed to you.

18. Avoid blowing on your food. Instead, wait patiently for it to cool down. Blowing on food causes some of it to splatter onto the table, the tableware, and on others.

19. Avoid picking your teeth with fingers, toothpicks, or floss. Instead wait until you are in a private setting, or excuse yourself to the bathroom.

20. When finished with the meal, place the fork and knife parallel to each other, with the knife blade facing the fork, and point both to the eleven o'clock position. The fork tines may face up or down. The knife blade faces in.

21. If you need to be excused but will be returning to complete your meal, place your napkin on your chair. If you are not planning to return, the used napkin is placed to the left of the plate and loosely folded. The used parts of the napkin should be hidden from view.

22. In your home and someone else's, be willing to help clear the table.

23. Always show gratitude by eating and finishing the food given and by saying "Thank you."

Social Dinner Etiquette

You, however, must tell everyone how to live in a way that agrees with the true teaching. Teach the older men to have self-control, to be serious, and to be wise. They must be strong in faith, in love, and in patience. (Titus 2:1–2 ERV)

In the same way, tell the young men to be wise. You should be an example for them in every way by the good things you do. When you teach, be honest and serious. And your teaching should be clearly right so that you cannot be criticized. Then anyone who is against you will be ashamed. There will not be anything bad they can say about us. (Titus 2:6-8 ERV)

---

1. Gentlemen are called to be respectful and kind, and one of the ways to demonstrate kindness is by assisting the ladies at the table. When taking a seat at the table, the man may help the lady by stepping behind her and pulling the chair out and then helping her scoot it back in again.
2. In some restaurants, the waiter or maître d' will pull out a chair to help the lady take her seat. Ladies respond by saying "Thank you."
3. Both feet are kept on the floor.
4. To get a waiter's attention, discreetly raise a forefinger or hand. Avoid yelling. Be polite to all those serving, and always say "Thank you."

Additional Reflection Verses

Luke 14:8–11 (WEB): When you are invited by anyone to a marriage feast, don't sit in the best seat, since perhaps someone more honorable than you might be invited by him, and he who invited both of you would come and tell you, 'Make room for this person.' Then you would begin, with shame, to take the lowest place. But when you are invited, go and sit in the lowest place, so that when he who invited you comes, he may tell you, 'Friend, move up higher.' Then you will be honored in the presence of all who sit at the table with you. For everyone who exalts himself will be humbled, and whoever humbles himself will be exalted.

Titus 1:7-9 (WEB): For the overseer must be blameless, as God's steward; not self-pleasing, not easily angered, not given to wine, not violent, not greedy for dishonest gain; but given to hospitality, a lover of good, sober minded, fair, holy, self-controlled; holding to the faithful word which is according to the teaching, that he may be able to exhort in the sound doctrine, and to convict those who contradict him.

1 Peter 4:8-9 (WEB): And above all things be earnest in your love among yourselves, for love covers a multitude of sins. Be hospitable to one another without grumbling.

Chapter 15

Church Etiquette

Biblical Foundation

Therefore I, a prisoner for serving the Lord, beg you to lead a life worthy of your calling, for you have been called by God. Always be humble and gentle. Be patient with each other, making allowance for each other's faults because of your love. Make every effort to keep yourselves united in the Spirit, binding yourselves together with peace. For there is one body and one Spirit, just as you have been called to one glorious hope for the future.
(EPHESIANS 4:1–4 NLT)

The goal of church etiquette is love, order, and unity in the church so that we may fulfill the Great Commission given to us by the Lord Jesus Christ. Matthew 28:19 (WEB): "Go, and make disciples of all nations, baptizing them in the name of the Father and of the Son and of the Holy Spirit."

1. We are called to respect the house of God because He dwells with us.

2. God is holy, and where His presence is, that place is holy. Leviticus 19:30 (KJV): "Ye shall keep my sabbaths, and reverence my sanctuary: I am the Lord."

3. The house of God is a house of prayer for all people to come and receive salvation, direction, encouragement, healing, and deliverance. Mark 11:15–17 (NLT): "When they arrived back in Jerusalem, Jesus entered the Temple and began to drive out the people buying and selling animals for sacrifices. He knocked over the tables of the money changers and the chairs of those selling doves, and he stopped everyone from using the Temple as a marketplace. He said to them, 'The Scriptures declare, "My Temple will be called a house of prayer for all nations," but you have turned it into a den of thieves.'"

4. We honor and worship the Lord when we arrive for the service on time, ready to participate in praise and worship. If this is a difficulty or weakness, like it was for me, repent and ask the Holy Spirit for help. If it continues to be a troubling problem, humble yourself, like I had to, and confess the problem to other faithful, trustworthy believers in your local church, and they will pray with you and you will have victory. James 5:16 (WEB): "Confess your offenses to one another, and pray for one another, that you may be healed. The insistent prayer of a righteous person is powerfully effective."

5. Our God is praiseworthy because He is holy, excellent, and mighty. True praise and worship open our hearts to hear what the Lord is saying by receiving the preaching of God's Word.

6. During the service, we turn off electronic devices unless using them to access scriptural references or taking notes from the sermon.

7. We remain quiet, listening and giving applauses at appropriate times when others are also applauding.

8. During the preaching of the sermon, bathroom breaks are kept at a minimum to avoid distracting others, and they are always left clean for others. Eating is only permitted in designated areas.

Additional Reflection Verses

Exodus 25:8 (NKJV): And let them make Me a sanctuary, that I may dwell among them.

Psalm 100:3–4 (KJV): Know ye that the Lord he is God: it is he that hath made us, and not we ourselves; we are his people, and the sheep of his pasture. Enter into his gates with thanksgiving, and into his courts with praise: be thankful unto him, and bless his name.

Chapter 16

International Etiquette

Biblical Foundation

Let your gentle behaviour be clear to
all men. The Lord is near.
(PHILIPPIANS 4:5 BBE)

Travel Etiquette

Good manners and good judgment are important when traveling to another country. Leave a great impression by always representing the country you come from well. Keep praying and asking the Holy Spirit to order your steps as you do your research on the country you are traveling to. Research the culture, customs, and laws. You don't want to come across as disrespectful, arrogant, and indifferent.

1. Download a language translation application on your phone or purchase a dictionary for the national or official language of the country you are visiting.
2. Find out if you need a visa. Go to the country's embassy website and confirm.

3. Make sure your passport is current. Many countries want at least six months before expiring.
4. Check the weather advisory during the time you will be visiting.
5. For up-to-date travel advisories by the United States government, United States citizens and residents can go to https://travel.state.gov/content/travel/en/international-travel.html.
6. Before booking your flight and hotel, take time to read the reviews of previous travelers.
7. Use the traveling miles offered by your credit card company.
8. Always let others know where you are going, with whom, and for how long.
9. Know where the nearest embassy or consulate of the country where you reside is located.
10. Be patient. Learn a few phrases of the foreign language. People appreciate the effort and respect and will go out of their way to help you.
11. Observe local laws. No illegal or offensive behavior.
12. Tourists are easy to spot and can be easy targets for exorbitant pricing on cheap items. Resist accepting the first price; be willing to negotiate prices and even walk away. Unless you're interested, keep walking when people come up to you at the airport or hotel to get you to sign up for time-shares. They'll entice you with promises of free dinners and free tours. Always research other tourists' experiences.
13. Tipping is common in many countries.
14. Stay respectful and humble before the locals, appreciating the beauty of their country and culture.
15. Smile a lot and keep a great and thankful attitude. It is much easier to help a friendly person than an obnoxious one.
16. Have fun!

My husband has been practicing pediatric medicine with three doctors of Indian heritage for many years, and as a result, we have become quite knowledgeable about the Indian culture. In addition, we have had the great pleasure of traveling to parts of Asia and the Middle East, specifically Turkey, the United Arab Emirates, and Israel. Let's take a look at two countries—India, in Asia, and Israel, in the Middle East—and their unique etiquette.

Indian Etiquette

India is located in South Asia. It's the seventh largest country in the world, with a population of over 1.2 billion people. New Delhi is its capital city. The currency is the Indian rupee. The two official languages are Hindi and English. As a former British colony, etiquette is quite formal and conservative in India. Cricket is the national sport. The Indian population consists of mainly Hindu and Muslim, with a small percentage of other faiths. Status is often determined by caste, profession, education, and age.

Meeting and Greeting Etiquette
1. Only use the right hand when greeting. No other touching required. The left hand is considered "unclean," as it's used for personal hygiene purposes.
2. Much eye contact is not necessary, especially between subordinates and the boss or between castes.
3. Use professional titles, such as "professor" and "doctor."
4. Use courtesy titles "Mr.," "Mrs.," or "Miss" with the surname. Wait to be invited to use first names.
5. Use "sir" or "ma'am" for strangers, and "Uncle" or "Aunty" for familiar people.
6. When meeting a new business acquaintance, it is common to be introduced by another person, as business relationships are built upon personal relationships.

Dress Etiquette
1. Dress modestly. Loose, cool clothing that covers as much as possible is best.
2. At the beach, women are expected to be discreet.

3. In mosques and Sikh gurudwaras, women's hair and shoulders should be covered.
4. Men and women should not wear shorts, which are considered quite strange in Indian culture.
5. No shoes in places of worship, including some churches. Some faiths expect feet to be washed after removing shoes.
6. No shoes in some museums and historical monuments.
7. Business dress for men: suit and tie. Due to warm weather, however, a long-sleeved shirt with a tie is common.
8. Casual wear is acceptable in the technology sector and in informal situations.
9. Foreign women can wear pantsuits or skirts that cover the knees. The top should have a high neckline.
10. During social gatherings, foreigners may wear Indian costumes, which is respectful and a friendly gesture that's highly respected.

Social Etiquette

1. Public displays of affection are frowned upon among all Indian ethnic groups.
2. Avoid placing a purse or wallet in the back pocket.
3. It is considered rude and aggressive to stand with your hands on hips.
4. It is bad manners to point with the finger or feet.
5. It is bad manners to whistle in public.
6. When an elder enters the room, stand and offer them a seat.
7. A cup of tea is offered to anyone who steps into the home or office.
8. Always show respect by standing when the national anthem (of any country) is playing.
9. Avoid negative comments about another person's appearance.
10. In small towns and villages especially, be careful with expressions of social friendship between men and women, such as handshaking, hugging, and kisses. Follow what others are doing.

11. A religious object should not be touched with feet or the left hand.

12. Indians are loyal to their families and community. Great respect is given to the elderly.

Family Etiquette

1. Take off your shoes and leave them outside the house before entering the home.

2. It is good manners to arrive late by about fifteen to thirty minutes.

3. The men are left in the living room to speak by themselves, while the women remain mostly in the kitchen.

4. Indian cooking takes long hours, so showing appreciation and complimenting the lady of the house is considered good manners.

5. Instead of saying "Thank you," it is good etiquette to invite the hosts to dinner in the future.

6. When hosting a social event in India, it is important to call each person you've invited, even if a printed invitation was sent.

7. It is not uncommon for Indian guests to bring their own guests, as they believe they have a close informal relationship with you. Because of this, consider a buffet.

Dining Etiquette

1. Indians are hospitable people. Guests and their needs are of utmost importance. Any breach of Indian etiquette by the guest is usually ignored.

2. To Hindus, the cow is scared, so many Indians are vegetarians or don't eat beef. They also offer food to their god before consuming it.

3. Eat with your right hand only. It is offensive to use the left hand, as it is used for personal cleaning purposes.

4. Wait to be served by the host or waiter to keep from dirtying the serving utensils.

5. India is a large country, and etiquette varies depending on the region. In the north where they eat *rotis* (flat bread) and thick curries, for example, they use only the two right-hand fingers. In the south, the whole hand is used because they eat lots of rice.

6. When traveling within India, many Indian families carry a lot of food and will invite you to have some.

7. In restaurants it is customary to share the different dishes ordered with everyone. However, it is offensive to share a spoon, fork, knife, cup, glass, or drinking bottle. It is also offensive to bite a piece of another person's burger, candy bar, etc.

8. When giving gifts, be careful not to give any animal products, like leather, as many Indians are vegetarian or don't eat certain animals, like cows. Giving leather would be extremely offensive, as animals are sacred to many Indians because they believe they serve as transport for their various gods. Hindus believe animals should not be harmed; in fact, the slaughtering of a cow is banned in most states in India.

9. Avoid talking about how much you like eating steak and always buy and wear leather, for the same reasons mentioned above.

10. If invited by an Indian family and you're unable to attend, gently decline with a promise to accept in the future.

Business Etiquette
1. Stay calm, cool, and collected when dealing with government officials.

2. Appointments can be suddenly rescheduled or delayed for several hours.

3. Usual office hours are from 10:00 a.m. to 5:00 p.m. Some, however, start much earlier. Don't assume anything; always ask.

4. Subordinates stand up when the boss enters the room. Follow suit and greet the boss.

5. Giving business cards is a necessary part of business, so bring plenty.

6. At business meetings, restrain from jumping into work-related matters. Rather, begin with small talk, such as about cricket, family, and children. Avoid taboo topics, such as India's poverty, the caste system, immigration, and any difficult areas in international relations.

Israeli Etiquette

We vacationed in Israel for about a week in 2016 and toured Tel Aviv, Jerusalem, Haifa, Nazareth, and Jaffa. We befriended a Jewish taxi driver—David—who took a liking to us and offered to be our personal driver and tour guide. Israel is a beautiful country with a population of over 8.5 million people. Jerusalem is its capital city. The currency is the Israeli shekel. The official language is Hebrew. The most commonly used foreign language is English. Arabic is used officially for the Arab minority. The Israeli population consists of mainly Jewish and Muslims with a small percentage of Christians and Druze.

Meeting and Greet Etiquette
1. The normal way to say hello and goodbye is the same word: "Shalom," meaning peace. You may say "Shalom," then the person's name.
2. Use courtesy titles "Mr.," "Mrs.," or "Miss" with the surname. Wait to be invited to use first names.
3. Israelis stand close to each other when talking, so don't offend by stepping back; however, religiously observant individuals stand farther apart from the opposite gender, to avoid touching.
4. Give warm handshakes while maintaining eye contact, but be aware that it is forbidden for religiously observant men and women to touch each other. If unsure, wait to be greeted. If their level of observance permits it, the man or woman will extend their hand to you.
5. A religiously observant man would have a *kippa* (circular head covering). A religiously observant woman would wear a blouse that covers her neckline and collarbone, with sleeve lengths

below the elbow. Her skirt would be below her knees, and she would be wearing stockings with closed shoes or socks with sandals. If she is married, she may have a head covering.

6. Combining a handshake with a slight touch on the arms or elbow is acceptable among men when handshaking.

7. Maintain eye contact throughout conversations to show respect and interest.

8. Among family and friends, hugs are acceptable with kisses on both cheeks by both men and women. Men may greet each other the same way, by kissing on both cheeks.

9. Always use the right hand when greeting Muslims.

Dress Etiquette

1. Dark-colored suit with an open-collared shirt is common for men. Include a tie for formal occasions.

2. Business suits, dresses, or skirts and blouses for women.

3. When visiting Jewish shrines or memorials, dress conservatively.

Social Etiquette

1. Israelis are known to be extremely direct and to the point. They also use many hand gestures. Some see it as aggressive and demanding.

2. Conversations tend to be loud and intense whether in private or public, open or confined spaces. Speaking loudly is normal and acceptable.

3. Maintain eye contact when in a discussion, and use good listening skills, as Israelis tend to speak fast and express different emotions at a rapid pace.

4. Anything can be discussed, even with a stranger.

5. Open correction is not uncommon.

6. On Saturday, the Sabbath day, offices and stores are closed.

7. It is considered bad manners to smoke on the Sabbath day or near religious sites. It is especially offensive around orthodox Jews.

8. Drunkenness in public is offensive.

9. In public places with large crowds, you will observe and experience what may appear as aggressive pushing and shoving. Such behavior is not considered rude, and saying "Excuse me" won't work.

10. Pointing with the index finger is acceptable.

11. Upon entering a store, you will not be solicited or acknowledged until you approach a store associate.

12. Tourists are easy to spot. At a market, be willing to bargain for lower prices, and when taking a cab, ask the driver to turn on the meter to make sure you don't get overcharged.

Family Etiquette

1. Jewish family dinners are unforgettable, as they are lively, friendly, and entertaining. You may hear singing and praying. Do your best to participate. The effort is appreciated.

2. Keeping guests entertained and comfortable is important to Jewish families, so come hungry, ask many questions, and have a great attitude.

3. It is acceptable to come late by about twenty to thirty minutes at social gatherings.

4. Never show up empty handed. Quality gifts are appreciated. Bring wine or chocolates.

5. If invited to an Arab home, always remove your shoes before entering the home. Remember not to give or receive anything with your left hand.

Dining Etiquette

1. It may be offensive to your host if you decline their dinner invitation.

2. Always bring a gift, such as high-quality wine, beautiful flowers, or elegantly wrapped chocolates.

3. Avoid bringing cooked food, due to kosher requirements.
   a. Taboo foods include pork and shellfish, like lobster, oyster, crab, and shrimp.

    b. Mixing milk and meat products is forbidden, so after eating meat, avoid asking for butter for bread or cream for tea or coffee.

4. Avoid inviting a Jewish host to socialize on the Sabbath or other Jewish festival.

    a. Jewish families are proud of their religious heritage. If you're invited to a Shabbat dinner, remember Shabbat is practiced from sunset on Friday to sunset the following Saturday. After God finished creating, He rested on the seventh day. Jewish families observing Shabbat honor God by resting from all "creative work," according to Exodus 20:8–10 (WEB): "Remember the Sabbath day, to keep it holy. You shall labor six days, and do all your work, but the seventh day is a Sabbath to Yahweh your God. You shall not do any work in it, you, nor your son, nor your daughter, your male servant, nor your female servant, nor your livestock, nor your stranger who is within your gates." Creative work to be avoided includes checking social media, talking on phones, cooking, driving, shopping, cooking, etc. So please turn off mobile phones and other electronics, and keep them from sight the entire time during a Sabbath dinner invitation.

    b. The Friday night meal is a great feast, and hosts go out of their way to make it memorable and distinct from the other days of the week.

    c. Always compliment the lady of the house for the great effort of preparing the different meals.

    d. The wife usually lights two candles representative of herself, her husband, and their children; however, some families light additional candles for each child.

    e. The wife will wave her hands three times over the lit candles, then cover her eyes and speak the prayer of blessing welcoming the Lord of the Sabbath into her home. A few reasons why women have the privilege of lighting the candles:

    i. Women tend to be more involved in the running of the home.

    ii. Jewish women atone for Eve's mistake in the garden of Eden—when she extinguished the light of God—by relighting the candle that represents the presence of God in their home.

    iii. The spirituality of the home is mostly determined by the woman, for she encourages biblical study and prayer in the home.

  f. There will be singing, then everyone may be asked to wash their hands. Please follow suit.

  g. After handwashing, there is total silence until after additional blessings are pronounced over the wine and challah bread.

  h. Once the challah is torn and shared with everyone at the table, the speaking resumes and the dinner feast begins.

  i. After dinner, a prayer and song of thanks is given.

Business Etiquette

1. In business correspondence, use "Shalom" as the salutation and not "Dear."
2. Bring a small and inexpensive gift.
3. Because Israelis are known to be direct and to the point, they appreciate truthful people and abhor deceivers and pretenders.
4. Before any deal can be made, Israelis must feel they know you and will ask personal questions about you, your family, your birth place, your religion, and even how much you make.
5. Be punctual to appointments.
6. There's very little small talk at business meetings, as Israelis get straight to the point of the meeting.
7. Agendas are followed precisely, and meetings are short, as they only last until tasks have been accomplished.

Additional Reflection Verses

Deuteronomy 8:18 (WEB): But you shall remember Yahweh your God, for it is he who gives you power to get wealth; that he may establish his covenant which he swore to your fathers, as it is today.

Colossians 4:5–6 (WEB): Walk in wisdom toward those who are outside, redeeming the time. Let your speech always be with grace, seasoned with salt, that you may know how you ought to answer each one.

Joshua 1:9 (WEB): Haven't I commanded you? Be strong and courageous. Don't be afraid. Don't be dismayed, for Yahweh your God is with you wherever you go.

John 10:9 (WEB): I am the door. If anyone enters in by me, he will be saved, and will go in and go out, and will find pasture.

Chapter 17

Benefits of Good Manners God's Way

Biblical Foundation
*The way of the righteous is like the first gleam
of dawn, which shines ever brighter until the
full light of day. (Proverbs 4:18 NLT)*

In Genesis 37 we learn that Jacob's son Joseph experienced such jealous treachery from his brothers that they captured and threw him into a pit, then later sold him for twenty pieces of silver as a slave to the Ishmaelite traders. He experienced further betrayal by his slave master's wife when she falsely accused him of rape and had her infuriated husband imprison him. Despite the terrible odds, we find that Joseph did not abandon his godly character or compromise his faith in God. He continued to honor the Lord and serve others with his gifts and leadership abilities in whatever situation he found himself in. The Bible tells us that God was with Joseph and caused him to succeed in everything he did. People of authority noticed that God was with him and placed him in leadership positions. After thirteen years of slavery, God gave Pharaoh a dream, and Joseph was called out of prison to interpret it. Pharaoh was overjoyed that God had given Joseph the meaning of Pharaoh's dream and gave Joseph charge over all of Egypt.

Benefits for Obeying the Word of God

1. You will be a role model to all. Hebrews 10:24 (BBE): "And let us be moving one another at all times to love and good works."

2. You will grow stronger in God and in His power, and sin will not rule over you. James 4:7 (ISV): "Therefore, submit yourselves to God. Resist the Devil, and he will run away from you."

3. You will continue to grow in wisdom because you are willing to listen to instruction. Proverbs 19:20 (ESV): "Listen to advice and accept instruction, that you may gain wisdom in the future."

4. You will stand out and be known as a problem solver. Daniel 1:20 (KJV): "And in all matters of wisdom and understanding, that the king enquired of them, he found them ten times better than all the magicians and astrologers that were in all his realm."

5. You will win favor with God and man, leading to promotion and greater responsibility. First Samuel 2:26 (NLT): "Meanwhile, the boy Samuel grew taller and grew in favor with the LORD and with the people." Samuel was found growing, learning, and serving the Lord in His house.

6. You will have a good name. Proverbs 22:1 (BBE): "A good name is more to be desired than great wealth, and to be respected is better than silver and gold."

7. You will win the confidence, respect, and trust of others. Proverbs 3:3–4 (ISV): "Do not let gracious love and truth leave you. Bind them around your neck, write them on the tablet

of your heart, and find favor and a good reputation with God and men."

8. You will have a happier, more successful life because you seek and maintain peace. Job 22:21 (ISV): "Get to know God, and you will be at peace with him, and then prosperity will come to you."

9. You will attract good. Seeds of goodness reap a harvest of goodness. Galatians 6:7 (ESV): "Do not be deceived: God is not mocked, for whatever one sows, that will he also reap."

10. You will lead a healthier, more satisfying life. Proverbs 16:24 (ESV): "Gracious words are like a honeycomb, sweetness to the soul and health to the body." Studies now show that bad attitudes and negative emotions (such as not forgiving, rage, bitterness, resentment, vengeance) are the source of many sicknesses and diseases.

11. You will experience stronger, better relationships because you are easier to be around and get along with. Proverbs 19:11 (NLT): "Sensible people control their temper; they earn respect by overlooking wrongs."

12. You will experience less trouble because you are willing to control your temper and watch what you say to and about others. Proverbs 21:23 (ESV): "Whoever keeps his mouth and his tongue keeps himself out of trouble."

13. You will have nothing and no one to fear. First John 4:18 (ESV): "There is no fear in love, but perfect love casts out fear. For fear has to do with punishment, and whoever fears has not been perfected in love."

14. You will always have the best counsel when you need it, and that comes only from the Lord Himself. Obeying Him results in greater confidence and faith. John 14:15–16 (CJB): "If you love me, you will keep my commands; and I will ask the Father, and he will give you another comforting Counselor like me, the Spirit of Truth, to be with you forever."

15. You will have the confidence and compassion to intercede for others because that is what Christ our Lord is doing.

Second Corinthians 3:12 (NLT): "Since this new way gives us such confidence, we can be very bold."

16. The Lord will fight your battles. You will have divine protection from the Evil One and his forces, and they will not overcome you. Psalm 34:17 (WEB): "The righteous cry, and Yahweh hears, and delivers them out of all their troubles."

17. You will remain undefeated. James 1:2–4 (*Voice*): "Don't run from tests and hardships, brothers and sisters. *As difficult as they are, you will ultimately* find joy in them; if you embrace them, your faith will blossom under pressure *and teach you true patience* as you endure. *And true patience brought on by* endurance will equip you to complete the long journey *and cross the finish line*—mature, complete, and wanting nothing."

18. Your prayers will be answered. First Peter 3:12 (WEB): "For the eyes of the Lord are on the righteous, and his ears open to their prayer; but the face of the Lord is against those who do evil."

Truly, the blessings and benefits of doing things God's way are endless.

Appendix

The Most Important Decision You Will Ever Make

Salvation is through Jesus Christ alone; no other founder of a religion died and rose again for His followers.

Acts 4:12 (BBE): And in no other is there salvation: for there is no other name under heaven, given among men, through which we may have salvation.

John 3:16 (WEB): For God so loved the world, that he gave his one and only Son, that whoever believes in him should not perish, but have eternal life.

Ephesians 2:4 (NLT): But God is so rich in mercy, and He loved us so much, that even though we were dead because of our sins, He gave us life when He raised Christ from the dead. (It is only by God's grace that you have been saved!)

John 14:6 (WEB): Jesus said to him, "I am the way, the truth, and the life. No one comes to the Father, except through me."

Isaiah 53:6 (BBE): We all went wandering like sheep; going every one of us after his desire; and the Lord put on him the punishment of us all.

John 3:3 (KJV): Jesus answered and said unto him, Verily, verily, I say unto thee, Except a man be born again, he cannot see the kingdom of God.

Acts 3:19 (BBE): So then, let your hearts be changed and be turned to God, so that your sins may be completely taken away, and times of blessing may come from the Lord.

Romans 10:9 (NLT): If you openly declare that Jesus is Lord and believe in your heart that God raised him from the dead, you will be saved.

Have you made Jesus the Lord and Savior of your life? If not, I plead with you to make the decision to do so now, and say this prayer out loud:

The Most Important Prayer

Dear Heavenly Father, I come humbly before You, in the Name of Jesus Christ, understanding my desperate need for the Savior and His Lordship. I repent of all my sins, and I ask for Your forgiveness. I confess with my mouth that Jesus is Lord, and I believe in my heart that You raised Him from the dead. Please come into my life, Lord Jesus, and be my Savior and Lord. Thank you, Lord, for saving me! In King Jesus's mighty name I pray. Amen!

Congratulations and Welcome to God's Family!

What Next?

Biblical Foundation

Hebrews 10:25 (BBE): Not giving up our meetings, as is the way of some, but keeping one another strong in faith; and all the more because you see the day coming near.

Psalm 1:2 (ERV): Instead, they love the Lord's teachings and think about them day and night.

1. Pray and ask the Holy Spirit to guide you to attend a church where He and the Bible are the final authority. At church you will hear and learn the ways of God and be encouraged in the Christian faith.
2. If possible, tell someone the great news that you are saved!
3. Get a Bible and begin reading it, even if you may not understand it all. You now have the Holy Spirit as your constant companion, helping and guiding you, and indeed He is eager to help you.
4. Receive water baptism by the guidance of your church leaders.
5. Receive the baptism of the Holy Spirit by the guidance of your church leaders.
6. Be willing to serve in your local church. The Holy Spirit will make it clear the gifts and talents He has placed in you.
7. Honor God with your tithes and offerings at your local church.
8. Continue with joy and trust in the Lord, for He is coming soon! Revelation 22:20–21 ERV): "Jesus is the one who says that all of this is true. Now he says, 'Yes, I am coming soon.' Amen! Come, Lord Jesus! The grace of the Lord Jesus be with all people."

The Conclusion of the Matter

John 12:48 (NKJV): [Jesus said], He who rejects Me, and does not receive My words, has that which judges him—the word that I have spoken will judge him in the last day.

John 14:3 (NKJV): Do not let your heart be troubled. Trust in God; trust also in Me. In My Father's house there are many dwelling places. If it were not so, would I have told you that I am going to prepare a place for you? If I go and prepare a place for you, I will come again and take you to Myself, so that where I am you may also be.

Acknowledgments

I thank the Holy Spirit, my Best Friend, Comforter, Guide, and Teacher. Without Him nothing great is possible. It was Him Who wooed me to my knees and to the cross two decades ago, and it is Him Who has kept me on the straight and narrow path. It is Him Who corrects, comforts, sustains, and encourages me to pursue impossible dreams. Hannah said in 1 Samuel 2:8 (WEB), "He raises up the poor out of the dust. He lifts up the needy from the dunghill, To make them sit with princes, and inherit the throne of glory. For the pillars of the earth are Yahweh's. He has set the world on them."

I thank God for my husband, Igho, who loves the people of the world and their beautiful lands and cultures. I have received much knowledge on etiquette and good manners because you continue to take me and our children around the world. You have also dedicated your life and medical career to bringing health and wholeness to all children. Thank you.

I thank God for my children—God's great rewards—who prayed and cheered me on throughout this project. I thank God for every child I have had the honor of teaching and serving. As a mother, aunt, and Sunday school teacher, children have taught me to forgive myself and others, to let go of burdens and just trust God. They have taught me not to take life so seriously but make time to enjoy and be grateful for the seemingly "small" things: a butterfly on a leaf, rose bushes in the spring, birds chirping, a walk in the park, tickling and laughing for no reason.

Where would I be and how could I have written this book if it were not for a sister who prayed and led me to Christ? Twenty years ago, my beloved sister and dear friend, Mrs. Rue (Ruguru) Watkins, discerned that I was spiritually sick, injured, and dying, and like the Good Samaritan, she loved me, nonetheless, to total health and victory in Christ. I thank you and love you for the example you have been and continue to be to me and to our entire extended family. Daniel 12:3 (CJB): "But those who can discern [are spiritually wise] will shine like the brightness of heaven's dome, and those who turn many to righteousness like the stars forever and ever."

I thank God for pastors after His heart. Jeremiah 3:15 (KJV): "And I will give you pastors according to mine heart, which shall feed you with knowledge and understanding." My pastors, Pastor Stephen R. Hill and his wife, Pastor Emilia Hill, of Spirit Life Church International in Southlake, Texas, have been married for over forty-five years and been in full-time ministry for over thirty-five years. They are loyal shepherds to the Lord and His flock, who teach the Word of God unadulterated. James 5:20 (WEB): "Let him know that he who turns a sinner from the error of his way will save a soul from death and will cover a multitude of sins." My pastors saw a writing gift in me and encouraged me to write this book, my first book.

I thank God for my personal editor, Mrs. Arlene Dagadu, and her husband, Mr. Lawrence Dagadu, who introduced me to Redemption Press, my publisher. Thank you so much for all your labors of love with this project, your patience, long hours, and attention to detail. You are both jewels, blessings, and shining examples of Christ's love and patience.

Last, but certainly not least, I thank God for my project managers, Ms. Colleen Jones and Ms. Kate Myers, and project editors, Ms. Dori Harrell, Ms. Sandra Byrd, and Mrs. Melanie Dobson, who gave such invaluable editing and designing advice and who worked tirelessly to bring this book to print. Thank you so much!

Order Information

REDEMPTION PRESS

CPSIA information can be obtained
at www.ICGtesting.com
Printed in the USA
BVHW072258250319
543613BV00005B/975/P